RIVER SONG

RIVER

SONG

A Journey down the Chattahoochee and Apalachicola Rivers

JOE AND MONICA COOK

The University of Alabama Press / Tuscaloosa and London
Published in Cooperation with the Historic Chattahoochee Commission

Designed by John A. Langston
Maps by Deborah Reade
Photographs copyright © Joe and Monica Cook
∞

Set in Trump Mediaeval
The paper on which this book is printed meets the minimum requirements
of American National Standard for Information Science–Permanence of Paper
for Printed Library Materials, ANSI Z39.48-1984.

Library of Congress Cataloging-in-Publication Data
Cook, Joe, 1966–
River song: a journey down the Chattahoochee and Apalachicola rivers
/ Joe and Monica cook.
p. cm.
ISBN 0-8173-1034-7 (alk. paper)
1. Chattahoochee River—Description and travel. 2. Chattahoochee River—Pictorial works.
3. Chattahoochee River—Environmental conditions. 4. Cook, Joe, 1966—Journeys—Chattachoochee River.
5. Cook, Monica, 1967—Journeys—Chattahoochee River. 6. Apalachicola River (Fla.)—Description and travel.
7. Apalachicola River (Fla.)—Pictorial works.
8. Apalachicola River (Fla.)—Environmental conditions. I. Cook, Monica, 1967– II. Title.
F292.C4 .R58 2000
917´.58—dc21
99-050992

British Library Cataloguing-in-Publication Data available

This book is dedicated to our parents and families,
who have encouraged and supported us in chasing down our dreams,
as unorthodox as those dreams may be.

Publication of this work has been supported in part by grants and donations
from the following agencies and institutions.

Chattahoochee Riverkeeper

The Georgia Conservancy

Georgia Power Company

Historic Chattahoochee Commission

Oxbow Meadows Environmental Learning Center / Columbus State University

Thomas M. Kirbo and Irene B. Kirbo Charitable Trust

Upper Chattahoochee Riverkeeper

Contents

CHATTAHOOCHEE DREAMING   5

HEADWATERS   15

NACOOCHEE   33

SIDNEY LANIER'S LEGACY   51

NORTH ATLANTA'S SPRAWL   71

LIFE ON "DEAD RIVER"   89

WATER OVER THE DAMS   109

PICKING ON ALABAMA   127

CRITTERS   147

FISHERMEN   167

NATIVE ROOTS 191

THE RIVER'S MAYBERRYS 211

SPIRITS OF STEAM 233

WATER IS FOR FIGHTING 253

UNFINISHED BUSINESS 275

Acknowledgments 285

Notes on Photographs 289

RIVER SONG

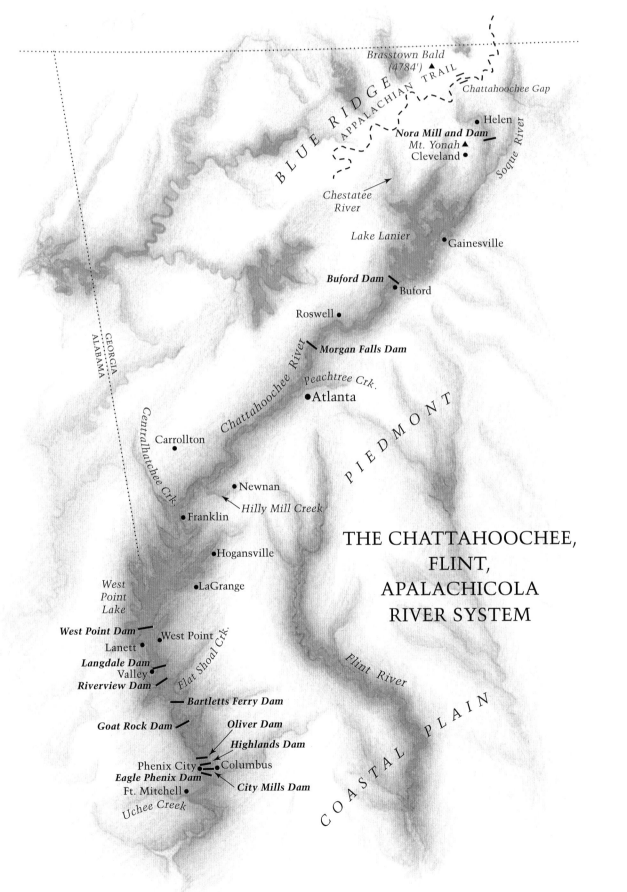

Brasstown Bald
(4784') ▲

Chattahoochee Gap

BLUE RIDGE

APPALACHIAN TRAIL

• Helen

Nora Mill and Dam
Mt. Yonah ▲
Cleveland •

Soque River

*Chestatee
River*

Lake Lanier
• Gainesville

Buford Dam
• Buford

Roswell •

Chattahoochee River

Morgan Falls Dam

Peachtree Crk.

•Atlanta

PIEDMONT

Centralhatchee Crk.

Carrollton •

• Newnan

→ *Hilly Mill Creek*

• Franklin

•Hogansville

THE CHATTAHOOCHEE,
FLINT,
APALACHICOLA
RIVER SYSTEM

*West
Point
Lake*

•LaGrange

Flint River

West Point Dam
• West Point

Lanett •

Flat Shoal Crk.

Langdale Dam
Valley •

Riverview Dam

— ***Bartletts Ferry Dam***

Goat Rock Dam   ***Oliver Dam***

Highlands Dam

Phenix City •   • Columbus

Eagle Phenix Dam

Ft. Mitchell •   ***City Mills Dam***

Uchee Creek

COASTAL PLAIN

GEORGIA
ALABAMA

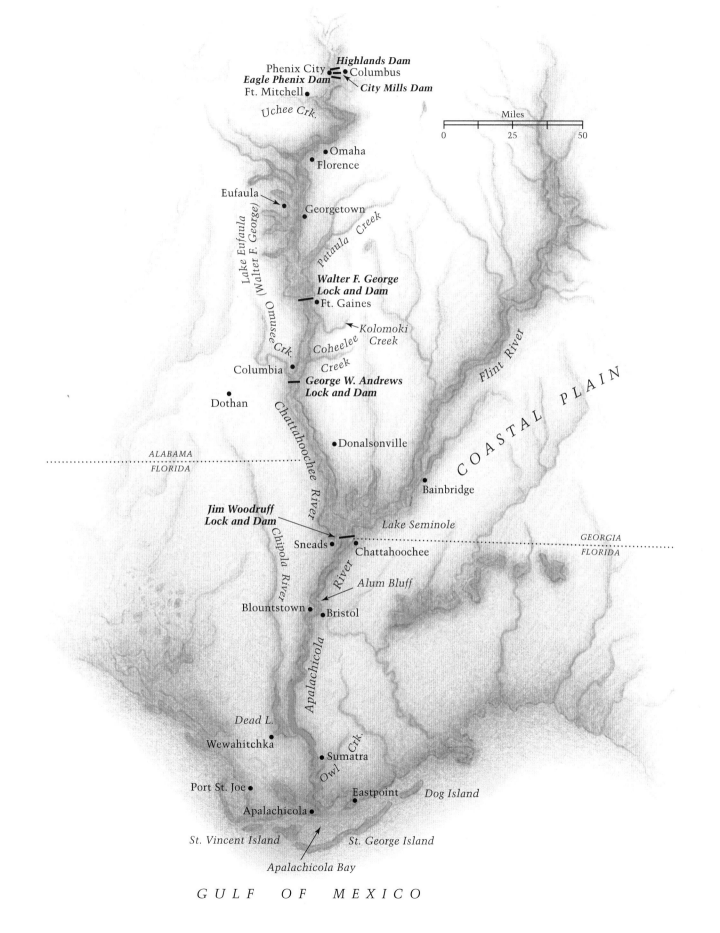

Highlands Dam
Phenix City
Eagle Phenix Dam
Ft. Mitchell
City Mills Dam
Columbus

Uchee Crk.

Miles
0   25   50

Omaha
Florence

Eufaula
Georgetown

Lake Eufaula (Walter F. George)

Pataula Creek

Walter F. George
Lock and Dam
Ft. Gaines

Omusee Crk.

Kolomoki Creek

Coheelee Creek

Flint River

COASTAL PLAIN

Columbia
George W. Andrews
Lock and Dam

Dothan

Chattahoochee River

Donalsonville

ALABAMA
FLORIDA

Bainbridge

Jim Woodruff
Lock and Dam

Lake Seminole

GEORGIA
FLORIDA

Sneads
Chattahoochee

Chipola River

River

Alum Bluff

Blountstown
Bristol

Apalachicola

Dead L.

Wewahitchka

Owl Crk.

Sumatra

Port St. Joe

Eastpoint

Dog Island

Apalachicola

St. Vincent Island

St. George Island

Apalachicola Bay

GULF   OF   MEXICO

ABOVE: *Joe in the mist below Buford Dam*
FACING PAGE: *Joe and Monica at the beginning of their journey*

CHAPTER ONE

CHATTAHOOCHEE DREAMING

It was April 2, 1995, and the second day of our source-to-sea journey on the Chattahoochee and Apalachicola Rivers. We had some 535 miles ahead of us to reach the river's mouth on the Gulf of Mexico, and the better part of three months set aside to accomplish the feat. Burdened with full packs, we bushwhacked along the young Chattahoochee's course as it winds its way through the Chattahoochee National Forest of north Georgia. It would be another day and a half of foot travel before the river grew large enough to float our canoe.

Already, the journey was surprising us. We didn't expect such rugged terrain or the tremendous waterfalls that we cautiously stepped through, around, and over. It wasn't long before we began to question the wisdom of our journey.

Rounding one wild bend where we had to shout over the roar of the water to hear each other, we ran into a pair of fishermen. We asked them if the river's course got gentler further downstream, and they looked at us bewildered.

"I went in there once," said one fisherman as he pointed to the deepening gorge. "I fell on a rock and busted my knee cap. It took me seven hours to get out to a hospital. I can give you a ride to the other side. My truck's just at the top of the hill."

Still determined to follow the river, we replied, "No thanks, we'd rather walk."

"Ooooooooh," he said, seemingly enlightened about our grand endeavor. "You're into that Blue Highway crap, that Walk Across America stuff."

Monica and I just looked at each other and laughed. We'd read both of the adventure travel novels the fisherman was referring to when we were impressionable college students. No doubt those exciting tales of long-distance journeys had influenced us and helped bring us to this wild spot along the river on an adventure of our own. Had we not been in a hurry to get through the gorge, we would have told our full story to the insightful fisherman.

This journey really has its beginnings in our childhoods. We grew up children of Atlanta's suburbs, sustained by Chattahoochee River water. We were raised in its watershed. We played in it and its tributaries, we picnicked at its shores, we soaked up its beauty and its cool water.

Yet the bond with the river was hardly confined to aesthetics. It was, very literally, our life support. It came through the pipes in our suburban homes, cleaned our bodies as infants, quenched our thirsts on summer nights spent playing kick-the-can, and watered the lawn that we begrudgingly mowed as teenagers.

But even in our childhood there existed a peculiar dichotomy about this river. The river was our inspiration and our sustenance, but at times it had a repulsive nature. For instance, Monica's first memories of the river are of family picnics at the relatively pristine and picturesque Jones Bridge Park in the far northern reaches of Atlanta's suburbs. But my earliest memories of the river revolve around the distinct aroma of raw sewage and river water that emanated from the river in south Metro Atlanta. The church my family attended sat just a stone's throw from the

TOP: An Appalachian Trail marker points the way to Chattahoochee Spring
BOTTOM: Signs at Chat Rat Island erected by riverside dwellers in White County

river and from two of Atlanta's largest wastewater treatment plants. On thick-aired summer days, the smell of stewing sewage would occasionally seep into our church's sanctuary. Because of this unpleasant pall, my family and friends began to call the river "Chattamanasty."

In the late 1960s and early 1970s, the nickname fit. Raw sewage was regularly dumped into the river. In 1965, more than 20 million gallons of untreated sewage were released to the river

The Chattahoochee in north Fulton County winding past the Atlanta city skyline

each day from Atlanta's main treatment facility. The extent of the pollution was alarming.

By 1972, Georgia's legendary U.S. senator Herman Talmadge was telling reporters, "If we are to save the Chattahoochee from meeting the same ugly fate as most of the nation's other major rivers, then we must act now to evaluate the situation."

Jimmy Carter, at the time governor of Georgia, witnessing the tremendous land development threatening the river in north Atlanta, said, "This is a fight to protect our right and the right of future generations to enjoy the beauty of the river. That beauty can be destroyed just as easily with beer cans and garbage as with office parks and apartments, and it will be destroyed unless

each individual who comes to enjoy the Chattahoochee is willing to make a personal effort to preserve what has been entrusted to him."

This is the backdrop that shaped our relationship with the Chattahoochee. In fact the dream of following the river was born during that era as I played on a Chattahoochee tributary that my family called Snake Creek. On it I built my first dam, caught my first crawfish and spooked my first snake. It was the only wilderness available in our suburb.

One day my creeking buddy, Andrew Groover, and I set out to follow the stream. We had a vague idea of where it led, but we'd never ventured far on this natural path. It was an all-day affair—or at least that's the way I remember it.

The creek widened and passed from home lot to woods to pasture and finally it reached the Chattahoochee. By the time we reached our destination, we were muddy and wet but thrilled with the adventure. In those moments of the late afternoon, as we squeaked back home in wet sneakers, my mind began to wander downriver to adventures yet remaining.

In some way the journey made me aware for the first time that I was part of a bigger picture. My world as a twelve-year-old was small, about the size of Snake Creek's drainage basin, but in making our grand adventure, the mud and water moving about our feet taught us a lesson. Like the water before us, we were hurtling toward life's mainstream. Though we seemed insignificant at the time, the creek showed us we might some day make mighty movements like so many tiny creeks creating a surging river.

It was not a traditionally significant moment like one's first little league game or first kiss, but today, I remember it as well as that awkward kiss on the top bleachers in the middle school gym.

Some fifteen years later, in the spring of 1992, Monica and I camped at Chattahoochee Gap along the Appalachian Trail in north Georgia where a spring first gives life to the Chattahoochee.

We were on the fifth day of a thousand mile backpacking trip that would take us to Pennsylvania, where we had stopped the previous year on our southbound journey from the Trail's other end at Mt. Katahdin in Maine. Just ten days before this night at the Gap we had been married, and we were filled with the excitement and optimism that comes with being honeymooners.

As we talked over dinner, I recalled my childhood dream of following the river's course, and Monica suggested, "If a person can hike 2,000

miles on the Appalachian Trail, surely we could hike and canoe 500 miles on the Chattahoochee."

"I suppose so," I said, but my mind was still on the 1,000 miles ahead of us on the Trail. We slept soundly that night and still remember it as the best night's sleep we've ever enjoyed on the Trail. A grouse thumped in the early morning, searching for a mate, and in our deep slumber we must have dreamed of the river.

Several days later we escaped the mountains for a shower and warm bed at Rainbow Springs Campground in North Carolina where we ran into Lisa Pirkle a short, spirited woman who was vacationing with her two boys in the cabin next door. When we mentioned our night at Chattahoochee Gap, she immediately produced a sheaf of literature about the river and its many troubles. It was one of those serendipitous moments that Appalachian Trail hikers refer to as "trail magic." The dream of following the river might well have been permanently filed in the big mental folder labeled "future plans," had it not been for this chance encounter with a vacationing environmental activist from Atlanta. Immediately we saw a purpose in a source-to-sea expedition aside from fulfilling a childhood dream. We realized that we could use the trip to promote the river's preservation. Being nature/landscape photographers by profession, it was also the perfect opportunity to spend time in our favorite office.

In winter 1994, with the Appalachian Trail adventure under our belts, we began studying the river and planning the journey. Our hope was to connect with nonprofit organizations working to protect the river and turn the journey into a fundraiser, as well as a public relations tool, for these groups.

We set a departure date of April 1, 1995

Monica paddling through discharge from a wastewater treatment plant in Cobb County

(three years after our original encampment at Chattahoochee Gap), and began rifling through every book on the river we could find. We tracked down newspaper and magazine articles, searched for maps, and contacted individuals familiar with the river.

When we described our project, the responses ranged from outright incredulity to guarded enthusiasm. Margaret Zachry, the downtown development coordinator for the town of West Point, practically yelled into the phone: "People die down here on the river! Are you sure you want to do this?"

Sally Bethea, director of the Upper Chattahoochee Riverkeeper Fund in Atlanta, was more encouraging. She told us later, "I immediately thought this was the adventure that could help tell the river's story." Sally's enthusiasm proved essential to making the project a reality. She helped us form a partnership with her organization, as well as with the Chattahoochee Nature Center in Roswell and the Chattahoochee Riverkeeper in Columbus. With this support, we began seeking sponsorship from businesses that could turn a pair of financially challenged, beginning canoeists into a well-outfitted expedition.

Dagger Canoe Company in Harriman, Tennessee, pitched in with a seventeen-foot canoe, and by March 1995, ten more businesses had agreed to sponsor us through donations or discounts on products ranging from hummus mix to fishing lures.

While we prepared for our journey, the river rolled on to the Gulf, accepting the insults of pollution and abuse and, as we would soon discover, still maintaining its proud beauty.

The river's source, as we knew from our honeymoon trip, is a mountain spring in the Chattahoochee National Forest in Union County, from which the stream flows some 540 miles to the Florida Panhandle and Apalachicola Bay on the Gulf of Mexico. At 436 miles, the Chattahoochee is Georgia's longest river, and when the Flint River joins it at the Florida state line and its name changes to Apalachicola, it becomes Florida's largest river. Draining a river basin of 19,600 square miles, it pumps an average of 16 billion gallons of freshwater into Apalachicola Bay daily and ranks as the eleventh largest river in the United States.

Fifteen dams block its course to the sea, beginning with tiny Nora Mill Dam near Helen. Its final man-made obstacle is the mammoth Jim Woodruff Lock and Dam at the Florida/Georgia state line. Along the fall line that separates piedmont from coastal plain between West Point and Columbus, nine dams span the river. Of its 540 miles, nearly 200 lie on man-made still water behind these many dams.

Where our creations of concrete and steel have not confined the river in the mountains and piedmont, the Chattahoochee alternately runs through shallow rocky shoals and deep sandy pools. Its biggest rapids scarcely challenge experienced canoeists and kayakers but can quickly humble the novice.

Despite the numerous dams and lakes along the fall line, periodic rapids continue all the way to Columbus where in two and a half miles, the river drops an amazing 150 feet. Below Columbus, the river widens and slows as it winds through the wooded, moss-draped shores of the coastal plain. Though the river is often referred to as muddy, sand is the predominate dirt on the Lower Chattahoochee. Sandbars lining the river there rival the beaches of the Gulf, and on the Apalachicola, some bars are as big as football fields.

Joe carrying the canoe down the back steps of Bartletts Ferry Dam between West Point and Columbus

ABOVE: Cows crowding around a fence in the Nacoochee Valley to inspect Monica
LEFT: Tomatoes ripening in the canoe on the passage through George W. Andrews Lock and Dam

Formed when the Chattahoochee and Flint Rivers meet in the southwest corner of Georgia, the Apalachicola winds some 106 miles through the Florida panhandle. As it nears its destination, the floodplain spreads into a six-mile-wide matrix of tupelo and cypress swamps, blackwater creeks and tidal marshlands above Apalachicola Bay. The Bay, a shallow, super productive estuary, catches the freshwater at the river's mouth, and a semicircle of islands—Dog, St. George, Little St. George and St. Vincent—keep the Gulf's briny water at a distance.

In its journey to the sea, the Chattahoochee is threatened and tugged at from all sides. Campers and fishermen are loving its headwaters

to death. Land development in north Georgia and Metro Atlanta fills the river with the piedmont's red clay, while toxins from city and suburban streets wash into its tributaries. As it has for decades, raw sewage still enters the river through Atlanta's antiquated and overburdened sewage system. Dams that permanently altered this once wild, wet ribbon have replaced spawning grounds with artificial fisheries. Dredging operations required for navigational use of the Lower Chattahoochee and Apalachicola continue to disturb potential habitat for threatened and endangered species.

In 1996, American Rivers, the national river advocacy group, began including the Chattahoochee on its list of the country's ten most endangered waterways. The river also stands among the 40 percent of our nation's waterways that fail to meet water quality standards set by the 1972 Clean Water Act.

Meanwhile, close to three million individuals living within the Chattahoochee's tristate watershed fight over this finite resource. In addition to supplying almost half of Georgia's population with drinking water, the Chattahoochee is harnessed for hydroelectric power, agriculture, recreation, navigation, and wastewater assimilation. At its estuarine end, the seafood industry of Apalachicola Bay also thrives on its steady flow.

In 1990, quarrels over the allocation of river water came to a head when the states of Alabama and Florida filed a lawsuit against Georgia to prevent Metro Atlanta's suburbs from increasing their withdrawals from the river. Bureaucratic maneuvering prevented a prolonged court battle and resulted in a seven-year tristate water study. The study's purpose was to formulate a basin-wide water management plan to carry the river and its people into the twenty-first century. It remains unclear whether the parties involved will agree upon and abide by the study's findings. Though common in water-starved western states, battles over water quality *and* quantity were unheard of in the stream-crossed east until now. Clearly, the East Coast's first water war with its courtroom posturing sets an ominous precedent for other watersheds under stress as populations grow.

The Chattahoochee stands at the forefront of this unsettling trend because of its geography. Metropolitan Atlanta, with its three million residents, lies a mere eighty miles from the mountain spring that gives birth to the river. Furthermore, the city sits atop a hard bed of igneous rock which supplies little groundwater. Atlantans consequently rely on the Chattahoochee's headwaters for their water supply. No other major metropolitan area in the country depends on a smaller drainage basin.

Despite all of its problems, the river remains an enduring link to our native land, as I believe it does for many who were raised in its watershed. Coming of age in Atlanta's burgeoning suburbs, Monica and I watched as forests and farms around our homes yielded before bulldozers and backhoes. Land was little more than a building site, and no part of the landscape stayed the same for long. Today when we return to our childhood communities, we do not always recognize the places; but we always recognize the river. It remains constant—always beautiful, always flowing, and always providing life's essential element. When someone asks us where we grew up, we could say, "In Atlanta's suburbs." But a better answer would be, "On the Chattahoochee."

This intimate relationship with the river is ultimately responsible for our source-to-sea journey. It is what made a young boy dream of great adventure.

On July 9, 1995, we paddled at last across Apalachicola Bay, landed on St. George Island, and carried the canoe overland for a ceremonial plunging in Gulf waters. We had spent 100 days living out a dream on the Chattahoochee and Apalachicola Rivers. This book tells the story of our river adventure as well as the stories of the people like us who consider the river their home.

Students from Arnco-Sargent Elementary School at the boat ramp near Whitesburg

Horse Trough Falls in the Chattahoochee National Forest

CHAPTER TWO

HEADWATERS

FROM THE RIDGE-TOP TRAIL ON THE SOUTH FLANK OF JACK'S KNOB IN THE FAR southeast corner of Union County, we look south into the giant geological bowl carved by the Chattahoochee River. It's April 1, and spring hasn't yet reached the Tennessee Valley Divide.

From our vantage point we can see between the bare, leafless limbs of trees and trace the course of the young river through the Chattahoochee National Forest. In the distance the unmistakable profile of Mount Yonah looms at the head of the Nacoochee Valley and gazes back toward the river's headwaters where our journey begins.

Chattahoochee Spring does not attract the average weekend hiker. After all, it is nothing more than a puddle of water, and guidebooks generally suggest more spectacular places. Jack's Gap Trail leads 2.5 miles southeast from Georgia's Route 180 to the Appalachian Trail at Chattahoochee Gap. Some 200 yards below the Gap on the southeast side of the Tennessee Valley Divide sits Chattahoochee Spring.

On the opposite end of Jack's Gap Trail, some five miles northwest of Chattahoochee Gap, is Brasstown Bald, at 4,784 feet Georgia's highest peak. Each year more than 70,000 people visit that end of Jack's Gap Trail. In contrast, probably fewer than 1,000 make the short trek to see the river born at this end of the trail. In a sense, this disparity is the river's first insult. The Chattahoochee is undervalued from the beginning. The view from Brasstown is breathtaking, but the scene at Chattahoochee Gap gives breath. The river comes to life here and for the next 540 miles gives life to countless plants and animals and to millions of people.

Sally Bethea, director of the Upper Chattahoochee Riverkeeper Fund, accompanied us on the hike up from Route 180. It was her first trip to the spring, and as we scrambled down to look at it, she commented that the spot is relatively inaccessible. To river lovers like us it seems the spot ought to be set aside as a place of worship. It's holy and everyone should see it, we think. But for now, at least, the spring remains secluded, and the signs pointing the way remain simple.

A weathered and graffiti-covered wooden sign along the AT bears the words "Chattahoochee Gap," and a blue "W" painted on a poplar tree nearby directs hikers downhill to the spring. Thirsty hikers on the Appalachian Trail are the only regular pilgrims.

As we milled around the Gap before our descent along the river, backpackers began filing through on the AT. A few stopped to fill their water bottles. Most were on their way to Maine, attempting 2,000-mile end-to-end hikes. Early April is thru-hiker season, and when these hikers asked us where we were headed, we answered, "Florida." They looked at us as if we were crazy until we explained our route.

Members of the Georgia Appalachian Trail Club (GATC), who maintain this and other trails in north Georgia, reportedly discovered Chattahoochee Spring. In late 1932, a party of nine trail club members led by Paul Colwell of Blairsville and Warner Hall of Decatur headed into the

north Georgia wilderness looking for the river's highest source. This expedition marked the beginning of a long romantic relationship between the GATC and Chattahoochee Spring.

According to an account published in the *Atlanta Journal* during December 1932, the scouting party reported "that the highest and most northerly stream source of the Chattahoochee is a bold spring, or fountain, rising within 75 feet of the actual summit of the Blue Ridge at an elevation of about 3,100 feet above mean sea level, in the extreme northwest corner of White County. The geographical location is approximately 34 degrees, 49 minutes north latitude and 83 degrees, 48 minutes west longitude." On one point the article was in error: the spring actually bubbles from the ground in the far *southeast* corner of Union County. Shortly after that expedition, GATC members appropriately became the state's first riverkeepers.

In 1934, the Civilian Conservation Corps was building roads throughout the north Georgia mountains. One project aimed to connect Robertstown with Unicoi Gap via a road through Chattahoochee Gap, threatening the beauty and sanctity of the river's birthplace. Mrs. John Stutesman, the first woman to hike the entire Appalachian Trail in Georgia, stumbled upon the plan during her hike and blew the whistle. After her 1934 hike, she wrote the GATC to protest the destruction caused by the road builders. Investigating, the GATC discovered that excavation had not only desecrated the spring but that the road would, upon completion, level one of the club's early trail shelters. A series of letters and phone calls to the U.S. Forest Service ensued, and before the end of the year, the Forest Service had halted all work on the road "because of its conflict with the Appalachian Trail." The completed and abandoned portion of the road now leads up to the Gap, where it abruptly ends. Today it represents the only flat land in Chattahoochee Gap and makes a convenient place to pitch a tent. We slept on this piece of historic engineering in the midst of the Mark Trail Wilderness before beginning our trek downstream.

Below the Appalachian Trail, the river begins its drop to the Helen Valley. In approximately fifteen miles it descends some 2,000 feet in elevation. Shaded by hardwoods and occasional groves of mammoth hemlocks, it cuts through rock and weaves through dense stands of rhododendron and mountain laurel. As we bushwhacked our way through, wearing full packs, we learned quickly why mountain people describe the sometimes impassable riverside thickets as hells.

The headwaters is indeed a wild and inaccessible place. At the right spot, where the river roars over a fall and drowns all other noise, it is possible to imagine yourself as the only person to ever visit the place. In reality, the headwaters has a rich cultural history.

In 1900, George and Lula (Lou) Vandiver moved their family of five children to a south-facing slope of land near the base of Horse Trough Mountain and within a half mile of the river. Their small log home sat about two miles downriver from Chattahoochee Spring. George, who earned the nickname "Dandy," ranged his hogs and cattle in the forests where the livestock thrived on the forest's mast, particularly the area's bountiful crop of chestnuts. George shot wild game—opossum, raccoons, squirrels, and bobcats—and when he rode to Robertstown to purchase supplies, he often traded in skins rather than dollar bills.

Lou, who died at the age of 104 in 1979, is remembered as one of White County's most colorful residents. She kept house. According to one White County newspaper account, she "made

their . . . clothes, quilts, featherbeds, bedspreads, pillows, spun and wove cloth and made suits for her husband and boys and knitted socks for the whole family." Remembering her, friends and relatives repeatedly told us, "She could never cook for less than fifteen people."

Comer Vandiver at the Chattahoochee Methodist Church

The Vandivers were not alone in their mountain retreat. At least four other families put down roots at the highest points of the river's headwaters. The community included a one-room schoolhouse that served more than twenty children and a teacher who boarded with the community's different families during the school year.

George and Lou produced two more children, Comer and Fannie, on the headwaters. Both were born in the cabin overlooking the river. Comer Vandiver and Fannie Vandiver Lusk are now the only surviving children of George and Lou, and when we paddled through Helen, they were both still living there within spitting distance of the river.

Their recollections of their childhoods at the headwaters are sketchy, but one story that has survived the years appropriately revolves around the family's water supply.

Fetching water meant a long, steep walk to and from the watering hole below. To make the job easier (and in response to Lou's complaints, according to some accounts), George designed a pulley system so that the family could bring up water in a bucket without ever leaving the cabin's porch.

George and Lou now rest in a well-tended plot in the cemetery of the Chattahoochee Methodist Church in Robertstown. Their grave marker reads: "We are not dead, but just away." Their cabin was eventually dismantled and moved by the Forest Service. For some years it was reportedly used as a residence near Suches, but wood decays in the moist southern Appalachians, and the old cabin has returned to the forest duff. The only traces left by the Vandivers are a few chimney stones scattered on the ground near a Chattahoochee tributary now known as Vandiver Branch.

Fannie Vandiver Lusk

By 1913, times were about to change in the river's headwaters. That year, the Gainesville and Northwestern Railroad arrived with the primary purpose of transporting to Gainesville milled virgin pine and poplar from the Byrd-Matthews sawmill in Helen.

The raw logs, some of which measured twenty-five feet in circumference, were brought into town via logging railroads constructed into the secluded coves and hollows surrounding the town. One of the first lines completed ran up the Chattahoochee. Soon lumberjacks were methodically harvesting the best of the timber lining the river's banks.

Today's traveler can follow the route of the eighty-year-old logging railroad for about ten miles from its origin in Robertstown. Remnants of trestles and even some bits of rail can still be seen. The forest has reclaimed the old rail bed, but with just a little work, the track would make an excellent footpath. Still, the U.S. Forest Service is hesitant to take on the project.

District ranger Tom Hawks, a veteran of twenty-five years in the Chattooga District who retired shortly after our journey, explained that the U.S. Forest Service was reluctant to build the footpath because a trail would make it more difficult to manage the headwaters' annual throngs of visitors. Between 1985 and 1995, their number doubled, making the headwaters the most heavily used drainage basin in the Chattahoochee National Forest. Each year during the early 1990s, 250,000 people camped, fished, hunted, or hiked in the area. In 1995, 65,000 cars drove up Chattahoochee River Road.

Indeed, during our trek through the headwaters, all sorts of detritus spoiled our view. Empty tin cans left behind by thoughtless fishermen were the most common trash, and "Charmin trilliums," those fluffy, white blossoms of toilet paper sitting atop unburied human waste, popped up frequently. At campsites along the river and its tributaries, we saw compacted soil, scorched-earth fire rings, and gnarled stumps where the camper's ax had felled live rhododendron and mountain laurel to make green firewood. On one majestic hemlock overlooking the river, a hatchet-wielding camper had hacked the letters "A-X-E."

"It doesn't seem to affect the people visiting. They are used to going to places where there are a lot of other people," Hawks told us. "What it's affecting is the environment, particularly along the stream zones. It's creating silt and turbidity in the streams, and we're losing a lot of vegetation. It's the degradation of the environment that's the problem."

To help manage usage, in 1994 the Forest Service began developing campsites and sanitation facilities at three heavily used areas. Such developments reflect current trends in the management of the country's public forest lands. The camper's tent is replacing timber as the driving force behind forest management. The Chattahoochee National Forest, with its proximity to Atlanta and other East Coast population centers, stands at the vanguard of new approaches to management.

Despite codes published by the Forest Service and other conservation groups that tell campers to "leave only footprints, take only photographs," degradation of the river's headwaters continues. It remains to be seen whether campers and fishermen can do as much damage as lumberjacks and railroads.

The sawmill in Helen didn't last long. In its prime it pumped out 70,000 board feet of finished lumber each day, but by 1931 the accessible and desirable timber in the area had been depleted, and the sawmill closed. By the mid-1930s the rails of the Gainesville and Northwestern had been dismantled, and Helen became something of a ghost town.

Then came Helen's second boom, one that may ultimately have a far greater effect on the Chattahoochee than twenty years of intensive logging. The boom has its roots in the vision of a few Helen businessmen and in the artistry of local painter John Kollock. In 1969 Helen's leaders asked Kollock to give the town's buildings a new look—something that would set the town apart and attract tourists.

Kollock, who was educated as a theatrical set designer and had been stationed in Germany during his years in the army, looked at Helen's river and mountains and remembered the German landscape. He made a small watercolor sketch of an Alpine village and gave it to Helen's leaders. They were delighted.

"At the time I said, 'Nothing's going to happen with this stuff but it's fun,'" Kollock recalled when we visited him on the banks of the river near Helen. He was wrong. Helen became an ersatz Alpine village visited during the 1990s by an estimated 3 million tourists annually. At any time, a year-round population of 300 may be found playing host to 30,000 guests.

The Chattahoochee itself floats thousands of tubers through downtown Helen each year. The town currently houses the largest importer of European gift items in the country and continues to grow with new hotels, outlet stores, and vacation homes.

Kollock, a historic preservationist at heart, cut his ties with the town in the late 1970s. The watercolor paintings and prints of historic sites that he makes today record the area's history. Ironically, despite his efforts to preserve north Georgia's heritage through his art, his most lasting legacy might be a downtown development project at odds with the area's rich culture.

Kollock still keeps the watercolor that started it all. Neatly framed and in pristine condition, it seems strangely out of place among his paintings of north Georgia's historic sites.

John Kollock on the streets of modern-day Helen

"The initial purpose was to give the people a way to make a living," Kollock said. "It did that, but I regret too much growth. I didn't know that was going to happen. I was just a set designer. I thought where I stopped drawing, it would stop."

As Helen's sprawl, or "Alpinization," as the locals call it, creeps out from the downtown area and the banks of the Chattahoochee, local residents and landowners watch the development closely.

Lam Hardman III of Commerce, Georgia, is one of them. In 1905, Hardman's grandfather, former governor Lamartine G. Hardman, purchased land in the area that included the landmark Nora Mill, the Nacoochee Indian Mound, and the historic home West End, built in the 1870s. Run-

ning through the front lawn of West End are two stately rows of walnut trees that once flanked the narrow dirt road leading past the house and the Nacoochee train depot and into Helen. The road itself has almost vanished. Today, Hardman, along with his brother, John B. Hardman, and sister, Shell H. Knox, owns some 650 acres of ancestral lands along the river. Ask him about his boyhood summers spent splashing barefoot in the waters near his grandfather's home, and he gets a bit nostalgic.

"The happiest days of my life were the days I'd get up there [each summer]," he said. "The saddest days were when I had to come home. I'm old enough to remember when there was a dirt road going into Helen, and I have to say I liked it a lot better like that."

Lam Hardman III barefoot at historic West End

"We'd like to hold on to the land and pass it on to our children. We don't have any plans to develop it, but the question is, how reasonable is that going to be down the line?"

A couple of years after our initial conversation with Hardman in 1995, family members sold for development 300 acres bordering the river. Within a year of the sale, Helen's sprawl had reached the Nacoochee Valley in earnest. Riverside woods had reverted to swaths of red Georgia clay under the tracks of earth-moving machinery. A short time later, however, the Hardman family, with assistance from the Trust for Public Land, gave the state 175 acres, including the historic family home, to create a new state park.

Visitors to the state park will one day sit on the front porch at West End, and there they will see two eras collide. They'll look beyond the rows of walnut trees to the roar of cars on modern asphalt, and the question confronting the Hardmans and all the landowners along the river will echo from the musty, cavernous hallway of the old home, "Develop or preserve?"

Morning mist and hardwoods at Chattahoochee Spring

Maple leaf and hickory nut in Chattahoochee Spring

Beech tree and fall reflections near Robertstown on the Chattahoochee River

Snow on hemlock and rhododendron in the Chattahoochee National Forest

A "painted rock" in the Chattahoochee National Forest

Winter in the Chattahoochee National Forest

"The Shoot" in the Chattahoochee National Forest

Fall in the Chattahoochee National Forest

Morning at Chattahoochee Gap along the Appalachian Trail and Tennessee Valley Divide

Bull Shoals, Hall County

CHAPTER THREE

NACOOCHEE

SITTING ON THE GRASSY SHOULDER OF THE RIVER BENEATH DUNCAN BRIDGE in southeast White County, we watched paddlers emerge from a five-mile stretch of the Chattahoochee's wildest whitewater.

Like the other canoeists toting their vessels up the slope from the river on this warm afternoon in early April, we had shoulders and backs that were sore, but we were wearing proud smiles. We'd just completed Section III of the Upper Chattahoochee. Someone who didn't know better might have thought that we had just navigated harrowing whitewater—five-foot waves and seemingly unnavigable falls.

The truth is, as whitewater rivers go, the Chattahoochee is a pussycat in a mountain area filled with lions like the Chattooga and Ocoee. It is a favorite of neophytes, who learn on the river's playful Class I and II rapids before moving on to bigger challenges.

It made no difference to us that experienced canoeists consider the Chattahoochee a kiddie ride. Nor did it matter to us that members of the Georgia Canoeing Association (GCA) coached us through every turn. At the finish line we felt like Olympic champions. We had passed the test: we had paddled through Three Ledges, dodged the canoe-eating Rainbow Rock (a rock on which canoes had left smears of red, green, and yellow paint), and twisted our way through Horseshoe Rapid, all without swamping our canoe.

A month earlier, we'd hardly picked up a paddle. Our prior canoeing experience consisted of rides on placid lakes during childhood days at summer camp and a few practice runs on local creeks and rivers around our home in Rome in the weeks leading up to our journey.

When we told Carla Bowman of the GCA that we planned to paddle the entire length of the river with no prior boating experience, she was incredulous. Carla is an instructor who often teaches married couples in the GCA's beginner classes. She screamed through the phone, "Do you know what you're doing? You're going to kill each other! You know they call the tandem canoe the divorce boat, don't you?"

Following Carla's advice, Monica took the captain's seat in the stern while I paddled from the bow seat. The brawn should go up front; the brains and finesse in back, we were told, and sure enough, the system worked. In 540 miles, we never swamped our seventeen-foot Dagger Passage and never sought out any divorce attorneys.

I suppose it was cavalier, even foolish, to assume that we could make the trip with so little paddling experience. Perhaps we were like the stubborn paddlers John McPhee mentioned in his essay *The Survival of the Bark Canoe*. When he told his paddling companions that they must learn the proper paddle strokes, they were indignant. "The look in their eyes showed a sense of insult," McPhee wrote, "resting on the implication that every human being is *born* knowing how to use a canoe. The canoe itself apparently inspires such attitudes because in form it is the most beautifully simple of all vehicles."

I suppose we were blinded by the simplicity—the canoe's sleek lines and its lack of wheels, ball bearings, brakes, rudders, or sails—

and enchanted by the paddle. We have since learned that these graceful vessels can make inexperienced captains and first mates look ridiculous, and thus we have tremendous respect for those who have truly mastered the art of the paddle. No one is born knowing how to use a canoe.

But the Upper Chattahoochee's canoe waters, stretching from the Helen Valley of White County to the backwaters of Lake Lanier in Hall County, seem to breed canoeists. Those who live in close proximity to this ribbon of adventure can't get enough of it.

During our eight-mile traverse of the Nacoochee Valley, Mike Jackson, a nurse who lives near Gainesville, joined us for the day. Jackson is an unusual paddler: he doesn't know how to swim. The previous fall, he nearly drowned when he capsized without his life preserver at Three Ledges Rapid, a big Class II whose final ledge drops about three feet into a pool of foaming water. When Jackson traveled with us, he was just beginning to recover from the scare. He never removed his life jacket on this trip.

Jackson's companion during that near fateful trip was Jesse Steele, a senior at White County High School. Jesse is the oldest son of Bob and Joanne Steele, who serve as caretakers on some 260 acres of land bordering the river in the Nacoochee Valley and owned by the Montag family of Atlanta.

Caretaking is an appropriate occupation for the family. The Steeles have much the same sense of the land, and much the same love for it, as the Valley's original inhabitants. When Jesse was a toddler, he and his mom played often at the river. It was the boy's companion and a favorite one for a family that shunned electricity (and modern necessities like televisions and refrigerators) until Jesse was eight years old.

Jesse was three years old, riding in the bow

Joanne Steele and Jesse Steele

between his mother's legs, when he swamped his first canoe. He flipped into the Chattahoochee's icy water on a tame rapid made treacherous by a March flood. Joanne followed immediately, catching her three-year-old son as he hit the churning current. They survived the scare, escaping to the bank, where, with friends, they built a fire to ward off hypothermia.

"I got chewed out for it," Joanne said of taking her small son on a raging river. "But he did have a life jacket on, and so did I. He's never had a fear of the river."

Today Jesse tackles the Chattahoochee with the reckless abandon that comes with youth and skill. He's been known to run the river standing, feet balanced on the hull, poling down the biggest rapids. His home river is still a toy. Nowa-

Downriver we met Dave Gale, whose family moved to Helen from Atlanta in 1974 to open a canoe rental and outdoor shop. Before the move, the family did some market research by driving around Helen one summer Saturday in a Chevy Suburban pulling a trailer rack filled with canoes. On that day, not long after the release of the movie *Deliverance,* the Gales rented every canoe they had. They moved to the mountains shortly thereafter. Dave's mother, Anne, now a grandmother eight times over, still operates Wildewood Outpost and still totes sixty-pound canoes along with the young men and women who work for her. The Outpost puts about 5,000 paddlers on the river each season, making this portion of the river the most paddled stretch outside metropolitan Atlanta. The elder Gale's bond with the river goes beyond the usual recreational or aesthetic connection. "It's my bread and butter," she told us.

Dave is a contractor now and operates an outdoor clothing and equipment shop on the banks of the river near Nora Mill (ironically, on the Hardman property that was sold and developed after our journey). He grew up working in the family shop. When we crossed his paddle path, he was training for the annual marathon between Helen and Lake Lanier, a grueling forty-eight-mile race. He was up to sixty-five paddle strokes per minute. Dave and his partner, Rob Hand, won the race that year, completing the run in seven hours and thirteen minutes.

And we paddled with Gary Gaines, a Gainesville businessman, who is most at home sitting in his kayak on the Upper Chattahoochee. We celebrated our success on the whitewater at his primitive riverside cabin, where he'd left a cooler full of steaks, potatoes, and beer for our enjoy-

Anne Gale at the Wildewood Outpost

ment. Gary gave us a joke that we repeated often during our trip.

"What's the difference between an environmentalist and a developer?" he asked. "The environmentalist already has his riverfront property."

The joke fits the Upper Chattahoochee's landscape, where riverfront homes, weekend retreats, and no trespassing signs seem to go up with the speed of the river flowing past them. Shortly after our journey, a pair of Atlanta businessmen bought for development a large parcel of land just opposite Gaines's cabin and bordering both the Chattahoochee and the Soque Rivers. By early 1998 the developers were asking more than $40,000 for one-acre lots in the upscale subdivision.

Savvy realtors and property owners tack "for sale" signs on trees facing the river to catch the attention of paddlers, many of whom have the cash to purchase the pricey riverfront property.

Construction of second homes is the leading industry in the north Georgia mountains, as we saw during our voyage. Not a day went by that we didn't hear the groan of earth-moving equipment or the pounding rhythm of the carpenter's hammer.

Each time a new home goes up, a bit more of the river's wildness is lost, and more pressure is put on the river itself. Less forest and ground cover remain to filter out storm water, so that when the rain comes, more silt rushes down the slopes of the narrow watershed and empties into the river, fouling the water and covering the river bottom with dirt. Water temperatures can rise more dramatically in developed and disturbed land during such storm events. Household chemicals, lawn fertilizers, and pesticides are one step closer to the river as well. All these changes can have a dramatic negative impact on water quality and on the creatures, the finned and the fin-less, that depend on the river. For canoe campers like us, the new homes mean that the best camping spots are gobbled up and posted. An avenue through a once sparsely inhabited wilderness seemed to be fast becoming in large part the domain of the wealthy, off limits except to privileged landowners.

While owners of historic parcels have held onto flat arable land along the river like the type that forms the corridor through the Nacoochee Valley Historic District, they sold for development the steep, hilly terrain that dominates the river's course through much of White and Habersham Counties. As a result, many of the homes on these steep slopes overlooking the river are marvels of engineering and attest to homeowners' desire to be near the water. One house has a series of nearly 100 steps leading from a back porch down a precipitous incline to the river. The walk would wind a marathon runner, much less an Atlanta retiree.

Delbert Greear, a third-generation resident of Helen and a onetime canoe and fishing guide on the Upper Chattahoochee, has watched the transformation during the past twenty-five years. He is a math instructor at Gainesville College now, but in the mid-1970s, Greear and his wife, Nancy, spent part of their time living without plumbing and electricity by choice, while they guided paddlers down the Chattahoochee.

The Greears now live in a home built by Delbert on ancestral land in Helen. They have indoor plumbing, electric lights, a wood stove, and even a television. Outside are a passel of chickens and a pair of dogs, Beau and Sally. The animals running about might bring to mind a stereotypical hillbilly dwelling, but the family inside the home chafes at that label so often applied to residents of these mountains.

Delbert Greear on the river in the Nacoochee Valley

Though Greear speaks in a distinct mountain drawl, likes to hum folk tunes, and is fond of colloquialisms, he is equally at ease using five-dollar words like "nebulous," "entropy," and "ersatz." He holds an undergraduate degree in English and a master's degree in math education. And he can hew a wooden bowl from a slab of poplar with as much skill as the finest Foxfire craftsman. In the tradition of famed mountain poets Byron Herbert Reece and Don West, Greear does credit to his mountain roots. Contrary to myths propagated by urban visitors, the people of the Appalachians have never lived in a cultural or intellectual vacuum.

The Greears have raised three children on the Chattahoochee. While other families vacationed in Florida, Nancy and Delbert packed up Ben, Jake, and Cary in their canoes and went camping on the river. The children learned the river's features, and today if you ask them about "Ant Rock" or "Lunch Rock," they can show you the spot.

"Those were the good old days," Delbert told us. "Back then it was relatively unpopulated, but now its like a suburb."

Nancy recalled the time that Cary, their youngest child, complained about the construction and no trespassing signs appearing at traditional campsites. "It's not fair," she said. "They get to camp there and we don't."

The good old days are over, though, and the family begrudgingly accepts the changes. "If you let it bother you, it will upset you infinitely," Delbert says. "The woods are full of the bones of dead Indians who tried to fight progress."

The absence of unclaimed or public property in the Upper Chattahoochee corridor makes it less than conducive to long-distance canoe trips like ours. The prospects for camping spots are even fewer in the Atlanta area, where rows of homes and apartments line the shores. When public access exists, as it does in the national recreation area near the city, the National Parks Service does not permit camping. The prospect of fifteen dams, requiring twelve portages, and nearly 200 miles of slow, arduous lake paddling, does little to entice long-distance paddlers to the Chattahoochee either.

Canoe trails with established campsites are common in other parts of the country. Florida has dozens of state-designated paddling paths, but they are virtually nonexistent in Georgia outside the Okefenokee Swamp despite the state's vast web of more than 20,000 miles of rivers and streams.

While we paddled the Upper Chattahoochee, Gary Gaines, the environmentalist who had fattened us with steaks, potatoes, and beer, was scheming to create the state's first officially designated canoe trail. The twenty-three-mile path he envisioned would encompass some light whitewater paddling south of Duncan Bridge as well as the calm waters at the upper end of the lake. With the establishment of a 1,000-acre state park on the backwaters of Lanier and promises by the state to establish a canoes-only camping area, Gary's ideas seemed likely to become reality. Still, we quickly discovered that despite his efforts, the river remained primarily suited to day trips.

Despite the deterrents, a few adventurers through the years have tackled the full length of the river on long-distance canoe-camping trips. The romance and allure of a source-to-sea journey remains as persistent as the home construction that gobbles up riverfront campsites. During each of the many speaking engagements we made after our trip, at least one person would tell us, "I've always wanted to make that trip."

Henry David Thoreau once wrote in his journal: "For the first time it occurred to me this afternoon what a piece of wonder a river is— a huge volume of matter ceaselessly rolling through the fields and meadows of this substantial earth, making haste from the high places. . . . One would think that, by a very natural impulse, the dwellers upon the headwaters of the Mississippi and Amazon would follow in the trail of their waters to see the end of the matter."

Rivers pique our curiosity and summon us to their shores. As they disappear around distant bends, they remind us of adventures left unpursued. Those who have paddled the Chattahoochee's length and those who have merely dreamed of doing so share a wanderlust. Perhaps it lies dormant in everyone, a primal resource waiting to be tapped.

In 1924, Sam Murray and Lloyd Radcliffe, students at Georgia Tech, paddled in a canoe named *Mary Worth* from Atlanta to the Gulf. We spoke with their descendants, who recalled their stories of sunburn and rapids. Only seven small mill dams between West Point and Columbus blocked the course between Atlanta and the sea in 1924. Today twelve dams stand between Atlanta and saltwater.

In 1936, the Greear brothers, twenty-three-year-old Josh and seventeen-year-old Philip, decided to set a course downstream. The family lived on the headwaters of the Chattahoochee in Helen, and Philip would become the father of Delbert.

Gary Gaines at home on the Chattahoochee

Josh Greear died in 1993, but the younger of the adventurers now resides in a new home on the banks of the river in Helen that was built, of course, by his son Delbert. Dr. Greear, as Philip is known by the thousands of biology students he taught during his twenty-five years at Shorter College in Rome,

has made a career of studying the state's water resources. Early adventures on the Chattahoochee no doubt helped shape his life's work. In 1973 alone, he traveled more than 1,000 miles on Georgia rivers. His experience has made him one of the state's most respected conservationists. He took his last canoe trip on the Chattahoochee at age seventy-two, capsizing in the whitewater at Smith Island rapid. "It was the first time I ever swamped a canoe," he said.

The Greear brothers built a pair of plank boats, lashed them together, and, with the assistance of their mother and a 1918 Buick, carried the homemade craft to Browns Bridge near Gainesville to launch their expedition. They stocked their vessels with canned pineapple juice, oatmeal, flour, eggs, and a slab of bacon before setting sail.

The brothers tried using the river as their primary source of drinking water, but they soon tired of mud. "The river water we boiled the oatmeal in was so muddy it turned the oatmeal golden," Greear said. "This was July, and we suddenly discovered there was a good source of water up in the fields—in watermelons. We ate an awful lot of watermelons. I don't know how many watermelons we ate, but once we started looking for them we never failed to find them."

As we listened to Greear's story, we marveled at the tremendous changes that had taken place in nearly sixty years: dams, riverfront development, and bridges. Today you'd have to search long and hard to find a watermelon patch along the river.

An article in the now defunct *Atlanta Georgian* made the brothers into celebrities as they paddled beyond the young city. Most of the people they met on the river were ferryboat operators and rural black fishermen. Today, of course, bridges have replaced the ferries, and sharecroppers have likewise disappeared from the river's rural landscape, moving off the land to find jobs in the cities.

The trip faltered between West Point and Columbus as the Greears portaged around the many fall line dams, but their month on the river was memorable.

"We talked about it for years as kids before we actually did it. The goal was simply to go down the river," Greear said. "We didn't have any destination. We were just going down the river."

Part scientist, part historian, and part philosopher, the gray-headed Greear believes strongly in humankind's innate desire to be near water and to explore waterways.

"I think somewhere in primate evolution, perhaps prehuman, there was a time when we spent an awful lot of time in the water, in the edge of the ocean mainly, but also at the edge of freshwater lakes," he said. "Name me the mammals at low latitudes that are primarily hairless like us—hippopotamus, elephant, manatee, whale. They're all hairless. Why? The only mammals that are hairless at low latitudes are those that spend a lot of time in the water. . . . Why are we hairless? I think we spent a long part of our evolutionary time in the water."

Three years after the Greear expedition, Caraker Paschal and Minton Brady constructed a canvas kayak and a twelve-foot rowboat and paddled the two vessels from West Point to Apalachicola. They covered the distance in ten days, contending daily with mosquitoes and drenching rain.

Another documented long-distance canoe journey on the Chattahoochee didn't take place until after publication of Rachel Carson's *Silent Spring* and the environmental revolution. In 1972, Roger Rozelle and Steve Kuniansky, students at Georgia State University, loaded a pair of fifteen-foot aluminum canoes and pushed off from Helen. Setting a blistering pace, the pair pulled their canoes onto the beach at Apalachicola twenty-four days later.

The last such trip came in 1987, when Clint Williams, a writer for the *Columbus Ledger-Enquirer,* set out in his kayak. In his whitewater boat, he quickly became frustrated with the wind and waves on the river's many lakes, and he eventually leap-frogged over nearly 100 miles of the Lower Chattahoochee in a car. He covered the distance from source to sea in a mere twelve days, paddling more than sixty miles the final day, and finished the trip at Apalachicola with heavily blistered hands. It was not the journey he had originally envisioned.

Our journey couldn't have been more different from Williams's marathon. We averaged a little more than five miles a day. Of course, the river and landscape before us had changed radically since the early 1970s and the Rozelle and Kuniansky expedition.

On the Upper Chattahoochee in White County, Rozelle and Kuniansky ran into a fisherman who, foreseeing the future of his fishing grounds, told them, "If I was a millionaire, I'd buy all this river up and keep it the way it is. I've seen the river down in Atlanta, and folks up here are going to fight before they let this water look like that."

Though there remain smaller parcels that would be prime candidates for protection, it's too late for a millionaire to save large stretches of the Upper Chattahoochee corridor from development. While the students at Georgia State, like the family of Delbert and Nancy Greear, found the Upper Chattahoochee relatively unspoiled in the early 1970s, the river corridor that we found had largely been exploited.

On one of his many river trips during 1974, Delbert Greear, who had seen the abandoned and wrecked hand-built plank boats of his father's era along the banks of the Upper Chattahoochee, discovered a dugout canoe partially buried in sand near the mouth of Mauldin Mill Creek in Habersham County. The vessel, twenty-four feet long and two feet wide, had been hand hewn from yellow pine. It has since been traced to the Cherokee Indians and now forms part of the permanent collection at the Museum of the Cherokee Indian in Cherokee, North Carolina.

The canoe, possibly more than 250 years old, is one of very few Cherokee dugouts to have been recovered from southeastern rivers. It was probably used as a ferry and a vessel for short trips up and down the river in the Nacoochee

Philip Greear at Greear Lodge

Valley, where the Cherokee thrived between 1700 and 1725.

Viewing the canoe in its protected case at the museum, we found our minds wandering. We tried to imagine the Upper Chattahoochee landscape in the early eighteenth century, as the Indians knew it. Looking to the future, we wonder whether folks will pull a fiberglass-plastic composite canoe from the river's sand 200 years hence. What will they say if they do?

Winter at Nora Mill

Winter sunrise reflected on water in Helen

Clouds in the Nacoochee Valley, White County

Leaves at Smith Island, White County

Sunset at Horseshoe Rapid, White County

Poplar leaf on pool at Smith Island Rapid, White County

Mountain laurel near Amy's Creek, White County

Mountain laurel on a rock face, Habersham County

Morning on the backwaters of Lake Lanier, Hall County

CHAPTER FOUR

SIDNEY LANIER'S LEGACY

SOME TEN MILES BELOW DUNCAN BRIDGE, JUST INSIDE HALL COUNTY, THE Chattahoochee begins to slow. Shoals disappear. The river flattens and sprawls. As we rounded one bend just above Belton Bridge and dropped down a one-step shoal cutting a diagonal swath across the river, we heard the sounds of an outboard motor. A few moments later we passed fishermen casting from their johnboat, searching for the white bass that were making their annual spring run up the river. We had entered Lake Sidney Lanier.

For the next thirty-nine miles, we paddled hard across flat, still water, contending with the wakes of eighty-foot houseboats and thirty-two-foot cruisers and cursing the wind. As many a lake paddler has discovered, it seems that the wind is always in your face, slowing any forward progress.

Sidney Lanier in the nineteenth century celebrated the river in his poem "Song of the Chattahoochee," a melodic verse that has been recited and studied by generations of school-children throughout the river's watershed.

> *Out of the hills of Habersham,*
> *Down the valleys of Hall,*
> *I hurry amain to reach the plain,*
> *Run the rapid and leap the fall,*

Split at the rock and together again,
Accept my bed, or narrow or wide,
And flee from folly on every side
With a lover's pain to attain the plain
Far from the hills of Habersham
Far from the valleys of Hall.

Avail: I am fain to water the plain
Downward the voices of duty call
Downward, to toil and be mixed with the main
The dry fields burn, and the mills are to turn
And myriad flowers mortally yearn

The rhythm and rhyme fit the river. The words roll smoothly and swiftly off the tongue like water over a rock worn by nature's greatest sculptor. Had Lanier written the poem after 1956 when the floodgates were closed at Buford Dam, the poem might well have had a slower, more ponderous rhythm—one suitable for a funeral march.

When the current slows at Belton Bridge, the river's free-flowing life dies. Between Belton Bridge and Apalachicola Bay, the U.S. Army Corps of Engineers, builders of dams and dikes and canals, takes the wheel of control, and Mother Nature is relegated to backseat driver status.

We were told that the lake was beautiful, and it is. Light sparkling on vast expanses of water always inspires, but Lanier's beauty is Hollywood-esque. A man-made lake is like plastic surgery for the river. It is fake. To believe in the beauty of Lanier is to believe in mankind's ability to improve upon God's creation. I like to think that Sidney Lanier rolled over in his Baltimore, Maryland, grave when the politicians named this lake in his honor.

On the other hand, the central theme of "Song of the Chattahoochee" is the river's swift and unselfish service to humankind, not its beauty and wildness. In fact, descendants of Lanier who now live in West Point downstream claim that he wrote the poem at the request of a West Point relative who was looking for verses to celebrate the town's river-powered textile mills.

Perhaps nowhere else is the river's service to man more evident than at Lake Lanier. The 38,000-acre impoundment has transformed a rural, sparsely populated, agriculture-based area into an extension of metropolitan Atlanta. A relative who once ran a soda delivery route in Hall County in the days before the dam told us that his best-selling drink was grapefruit juice—apparently the best mixer for the moonshine distilled in the coves and hollows now submerged by Lake Lanier. Today you're more likely to find Chivas Regal or Jack Daniels served on the lake's $500,000 houseboats. Hall County is one of only 130 counties nationwide outside a metropolitan area where residents combine to earn more than $1 billion each year. (Another such community is Cape Cod, Massachusetts.) At The Point, a skinny arm of land jutting into the lake from the Chattahoochee Country Club, million-dollar homes jostle each other on acre lots so close together that you could play catch between their bedroom windows.

The lake has spawned four-lane state and federal highways to carry commuters to Atlanta and Atlantans to their water playground just forty miles from downtown. It anchors a $2 billion recreation industry in north Georgia. Its ample reserve supports the water-intensive poultry industry, allowing Gainesville, Hall's county seat, to proclaim itself the "Chicken Capital of the World." In its role as water supplier for metropolitan Atlanta, the lake has enabled the city's tremendous growth, for better or worse, during the past forty years.

Nearly 13,000 homes dot its shores. More than 23,000 boats ply its water. Ten major marinas and more than 7,000 private docks perch on its many branches. The jet skis and wave runners are too numerous to count. It is the Corps's fourth most visited water project in the nation and hosts more than 7 million visitors each year. "It's like managing a circus," one Corps ranger told us.

What would Atlanta and Hall County be without Lanier?

"Without Lake Lanier and its water supply, there would be no metro Atlanta, at least not the thriving urban area we know today."

"Well, it's given me something as a pastime, my boat. What would I be doing now if the lake wasn't there? I wouldn't have anywhere to go."

"Wouldn't be much of anything. I'd probably be working in an office in Atlanta somewhere if it weren't for the lake. It's the most positive factor for the whole area."

"In a word: it'd be boring."

"We'd just be an ordinary suburb and maybe the Chicken Capital of the World, but we wouldn't be the bedroom community we've become. It's certainly created a lucrative career for me. The majority of my client base is in Atlanta. They started out with weekend cottages and now they have permanent homes. Because of Georgia [Route] 400, the drive's so easy."

As we paddled through the lake's coves and around its 124 islands, we discovered a lake and a community struggling with overcrowding and overdevelopment. A $2 million study sponsored by counties and cities bordering the lake and released in 1997 confirmed the concerns that environmental activists had expressed to us during our trip. Water quality is declining because of nonpoint source pollution ranging from old, leaky residential septic systems to nutrient-rich

Lillian Hall

(and sometimes toxic) sediment running off the developed landscape.

We met Lillian Hall, a housewife turned activist, at River Forks Park in midlake, where the Chestatee and Chattahoochee rivers meet. Hall moved to the lake's shore in 1978 with her husband and three children. "Our biggest concern then was finding smooth water to ski on," she told us.

But by the mid-1980s, Hall's biggest concern had become finding clean water to swim in. The frequent illnesses that plagued her daughter were eventually linked to poor water quality in the cove where the family swam. The drought of 1986 revealed a pipe from a neighbor's septic system emptying sewage directly into the lake.

Hall became an outspoken advocate for the river and lake. Through the early 1990s she issued loud, persistent calls, demanding that public officials act to clean up the lake and strengthen water protection laws. Her politicking became so legendary that a colleague once jokingly accused her of getting laws passed with little more than "a micro-mini skirt and a cheap bottle of perfume." Hall, the wife of an airline pilot, countered, "It wasn't cheap perfume."

By the time we met Hall, she admitted that she was tiring of the fight. She was writing a pair of novels at the time, one of them the story of a burned-out environmentalist.

After years of participating in a water testing program sponsored by Gainesville College, Hall said she used the lake with caution. "I swim, but not just anywhere, not just anytime. We have a formula: don't swim near discharge areas, never swim around marinas, don't swim for two to three days after a heavy rain. Where you swim is critically important."

Many physicians in the area have long suspected a link between the lake's water quality and the ear, eye, and urinary tract infections that routinely turn up in lake users.

"The lake is aging just like we're aging," Hall said. "How long will you be able to use it as a recreation source or a drinking water source?"

Though the public has long perceived Lanier as a pristine body of water with its clear, blue-green water, the stories we heard from Hall and other lake residents were a reminder that no matter where you swim, you're always swimming in someone else's waste.

To avoid the wakes created by the lake's big boats on the wide open water, we hugged the shores, where flame azaleas bloomed overhead, brightening our path. Beneath us lay a ghost town, visible only on our recreation map, which detailed features of the lake bottom that had once been terra firma. We paddled over bridges, railroad beds, and old farms. In all, 700 families were uprooted because of the dam. Most of the homes were either moved or burned, but some structures remain. Scuba divers have discovered houses, tractors, plows, and cars on the lake bottom.

The old Gainesville Speedway sits under thirty-five feet of water at the edge of Laurel Park. Dunlap Dam, the area's first hydro plant, sits, still intact, eighty feet below the surface, just upriver from Thompson Bridge.

The submerged dam, constructed in 1908, spanned the Chattahoochee and was 500 feet end to end. The dam rose 36 feet from its base atop Dunlop Shoals and supplied Gainesville with electricity until 1936. Lake Warner, which it created, was the Lanier of its day. Electric-powered streetcars brought residents the three miles from downtown Gainesville for picnics and fishing. Turn-of-the-century photographs show boaters in coats and ties or wearing ankle-length dresses.

Farther downriver at Aqualand Marina, where mammoth houseboats fill long floating piers, we paddled up to *Sugar Shack*, where retirees Harold and Dot Martin invited us in for a drink. The boat was a modest home by Lanier's standards, just thirty-eight feet long and twelve feet wide, with only one bed but with many other conveniences, including a fish-finder radar.

The Martins greeted us, and while their television blared news of the Oklahoma City bombing, they told us their stories. They raised a daughter in Gainesville and have grown old with

Harold and Dot Martin with a vintage photo of the *Barbara Nell*

the lake. A month before our chance encounter, they had celebrated their fiftieth wedding anniversary. Harold, who had been a mechanic with the local John Deere dealership until 1986, said there was no place he'd rather be than on the lake. Dot, a retired textile worker, prefers tending her flowers but likes to come to the lake "when I have all my work done at home."

They showed us photos of their big catches—striped bass half the length of Harold's six-foot frame and stringers of crappie too heavy for one man to tote. In the mid-1950s, Harold saw the lake coming and purchased a kit boat by mail from Sears and Roebuck. It was a twenty-one-foot cruiser made from Philippine mahogany plywood, and when he completed it, he named it the *Barbara Nell* after his young daughter. But before he could get it on the lake, a work injury sidelined him.

"They closed the gates while I was still in the hospital, and I had to come home and spend eight weeks lying on my back in bed. I was dying to get out there, you know," he said.

In the early days, the Martins liked to pack up the cruiser and head to the islands for camping trips. "We carried our food," Dot explained. "We didn't plan on those boys catching anything. That was fun back then. Harold would put lights up in the trees [powered by a portable army surplus generator]. We'd have everything but the kitchen sink."

The Martins have been playing on the lake ever since, but in recent years carpal tunnel syndrome, emphysema, and a lung operation have slowed Harold down. His faltering health mirrors the condition of the lake he loves.

Nevertheless, each spring Harold is out, fishing the lake, hoping to find a school of shad and the stripers that feed on them. "I'm still waiting for warm weather, right now," he told us one January a couple of years after our first encounter.

Leaving behind the Martins, we paddled into the middle of the lake's southern end. A thunderstorm was brewing. The bright white mainsail of a lake schooner racing across the water contrasted starkly with the black sky. When thunder began, we looked for land, only to find that it lay at least a fifteen-minute paddle away.

Nervous energy pushed our paddling pace until Monica inexplicably burst into laughter. When I turned to remind her this was no time to laugh, I also broke into laughter. Her shoulder-length hair was standing on end like that of a school kid who had just hooked herself to a Van de Graaff generator. My hair was in the same condition. We felt like flashing neon signs that read, "God, please strike here first."

Rain and wind came, settling our hair—a natural styling mousse—and filling our canoe with water. We pulled into the shelter of Holiday Marina just as the rain began to subside, giving us a chance to bale out the vessel.

After crossing Lanier we visited Erwin Topper, the Corps resource manager for the lake. Topper is a broad-shouldered man whose physique reflects his German ancestry. He is typical of the Corps of Engineers lake managers we met. Despite their positions with an organization that, among conservationists, has come to be known as environmental enemy number one, those that we met were deeply rooted to the earth—hunters, fishermen, and paddlers. One is even a renowned botanist. In fact, Topper is by training a forester, not an engineer.

"I was canoeing and kayaking before you were born," said the thirty-year veteran of the Corps's Chattahoochee projects. "Until we find a better way to deal with the water supply issue, I'm satisfied with what we're currently doing. We might get smart enough one day that we can give up this business of destroying the ecology of the river basin from here all the way to Apalachicola."

While Topper continually juggles the de-

mands of the lake's 7 million users—a headache in itself—his biggest worry is Atlanta's demand for water. The Atlanta Regional Commission (ARC), the ten-county metropolitan area planning and development agency, projects that the lake, in combination with Lake Allatoona of the Etowah River basin and smaller reservoirs, will be able to meet the urban area's water demands through the year 2020. Once this milestone has passed, however, planners say that management priorities on the lake may have to change. At some point, quenching the thirst of millions may come before keeping the lake full for homeowners fretting over property values and boaters crying for play space.

Ironically, many of the lake users most concerned about lake levels owe their livelihood to the boomtown of Atlanta. By the same token, Atlanta owes its prosperity in large part to Lake Lanier. As Topper put it, "The fella that lives on Lanier and works in Atlanta wouldn't have a job down there if we didn't let some water out up here." Without Lanier, Atlanta couldn't be as it is today. While the city has grown up as a transportation hub, first with railroads and later with the airport, it is the dependable water flowing from the tailrace at Buford Dam that has built Atlanta.

Steve Haubner, a senior water resources engineer with the ARC, moved to Atlanta from Minnesota, the land of 10,000 lakes, and upon seeing the river that would consume his work, he was shocked: "When I saw the size of the river and how muddy it was, I thought, 'This is probably a big management issue down here.'"

Atlanta is a cactus among American cities. The city's primary river is relatively small and in its natural state would be inadequate to feed Atlanta's large population. Without Lanier, the

Erwin Topper and Lake Lanier, working for Atlanta

area would be water poor. With Lanier, it is wealthy.

Mayor William B. Hartsfield, who had both an airport and a gorilla at the Atlanta zoo named in his honor, knew as much in the late 1940s when he began lobbying for the impoundment. Familiar with the city's historic water woes, he envisioned Atlanta's postwar prosperity propped up by a huge bathtub in the Appalachian foothills. He knew water was power.

As early as 1866, Atlanta's leaders proposed pumping water in from the river. Until that time, the city residents had relied on springs, creeks, and rainwater cisterns scattered on street corners throughout the city. These sources were fast becoming inadequate, but few people liked the idea of pumping in muddy river water. Instead, by 1875 the city had built a fifty-two-acre reservoir on the South River from which steam-powered pumps could supply the town with more than 3 million gallons a day.

In the 1880s, an ill-fated proposal to drill an artesian well at the corner of Marietta and Peachtree Streets resulted in a hole 2,044 feet deep through the underlying granite that yielded a small amount of poor quality water and underscored the precariousness of the city's water situation. By 1890, the city had outgrown the South River facility, and the artesian well was soon pronounced impure by the city's board of health.

The following year, Mayor W. A. Hemphill, whose name was later permanently attached to the city waterworks, took office. He declared, "I believe that it is conceded that our greatest need is water—water that is pure and in full supply. Our supply must come from flowing streams and not from ponds."

By 1893, Hemphill had permanently linked the city with the Chattahoochee. By the turn of the century, pumps installed at the Chattahoochee on the north side of Peachtree Creek could send 20 million gallons a day to the city's homes. As Atlanta historian Franklin Garrett noted, however, the transition was not made without a fight: "The Chattahoochee River near Atlanta was usually red with the soil of cotton fields . . . , and it was not until the new system was in operation that people would believe that the river could be made drinkable."

For a while, at least, the city's water needs were met, but city leaders hadn't planned for drought. Periodic, extended droughts during the early part of the century at times left the river so shallow that you could walk across it and forced the city to build a small dam below the water pumps to round up enough water for continued withdrawals. The problems sounded a warning that went unheeded until Hartsfield began his dam campaign.

Hartsfield's lobbying was supported by both Cumming and Gainesville leaders, who lavished on Hartsfield gifts that included a leather briefcase and train tickets to Washington. With the help of powerful Georgia senator Richard B. Russell, federal funding for dam planning had begun trickling in by 1947. Construction began in 1950 and was completed by 1956. The floodgates closed on February 1, 1956, but it took two years to fill the reservoir completely.

During a drought in the summer of 1958, the *Atlanta Journal* celebrated the dam and Hartsfield's foresight: "Because of reserve supplies of water turned into the river by Buford Dam, the river has been in the full flush of health. Without the dam, Atlanta water users surely would have been on a ration basis weeks ago. They should give thanks for the big impounding system and the water it doles out every day to keep the river at proper level." Today Atlanta's Hemphill waterworks can pump 220 million gallons a day from the river. The river slakes the thirst of 70 percent of the metropolitan area's residents.

It is difficult to determine exactly what Metro Atlanta would be without Lake Lanier, but certainly the city would be smaller. The deficiencies of the area's water resources might have sent the growing population elsewhere, and Atlanta might still be a midsized southern city not the least bit interested in hosting the Olympics.

Instead, like many water-poor western cities such as Los Angeles and Las Vegas, Atlanta is built on an altered watershed, one that has permitted the city to perpetuate the post–World War II fiction that unlimited economic growth is both necessary and possible. It is as if, in the words of the environmental writer Edward Abbey, "gigantism were an end in itself. As if a commendable rat were a rat 12 hands high at the shoulders—and still growing."

At lake's end, we made our first major portage, pulling our canoe out above the dam, toting it across Buford Dam Road, and then sliding it sled style down the dam's grassy backside. We were happy to return to a flowing river. The lake had left us with mixed emotions. We were bitter about the river's damming and its often negative consequences, but as children of Atlanta, we were grateful that the lake had been there to meet our needs.

Topper, the broad-shouldered leisure services manager, summed it up: "More than 80 percent of our bodies is water, and in my case all that is Lake Lanier water. I suppose if you squeezed me real hard, all you'd get would be lake water."

A million or more Atlantans might have said the same thing.

Morning at Lula Bridge on Lake Lanier

Afternoon reflections, Habersham County

Dogwood on Lake Lanier, Hall County

Sycamore tree near Mud Creek, Hall County

Sycamore leaves near Snake Creek, Cobb County

Shoals at James Creek, Forsyth County

Bluff at Hutchins Farm Road, Gwinnett County

Spring growth at Hutchins Farm Road, Gwinnett County

Fall at Medlock Bridge, Gwinnett County

Morning moon at River Forks Park, Lake Lanier

Sunset on Bull Sluice Lake, Fulton County

CHAPTER FIVE

NORTH ATLANTA'S SPRAWL

WHERE JAMES CREEK'S LOAD OF MURKY BROWN WATER MIXES WITH THE BLUE green of the Chattahoochee in Forsyth County about three miles below Buford Dam, we pulled our canoe up to the shore alongside a trout-fishing bartender from Atlanta.

"This is the spot where they want to build the Outer Perimeter," we said.

"Oh? That's a bad idea," said the fisherman, who appeared more interested in fish than in conversation. He paused, cast his line, and looked around. A thin fog hung on the surface of the cold water rushing by his feet, and a canopy of freshly green trees arced overhead. The air was filled with the sounds of the water. "That's a *very* bad idea."

The Outer Perimeter, a proposed four-lane highway circling Atlanta, would cut a seventy-mile swath across the city's sprawling northern suburbs, linking them while relieving traffic congestion on the original perimeter highway some twenty-five miles closer to Atlanta.

The original perimeter had been completed in 1969 for the same reasons—the need to link Atlanta's sprawling suburbs and the need to relieve traffic congestion on the city's surface streets. "Perimeter" is a misnomer, however. Far from defining an outer *boundary*, the road merely sets a new limit to be exceeded, and Atlanta's growth seems boundless.

In the twenty-six years since the dedication of Atlanta's original perimeter highway, the city's population has doubled. The majority of the metropolitan population now lives outside the perimeter, not inside.

The Chattahoochee, bisected by lines designating the proposed perimeter highway on state Department of Transportation planning maps, sits in the path of the sprawl.

For the next forty-five miles, we paddled toward Atlanta, home, and our childhood memories and through a landscape that has changed more, while being the subject of more controversy, than any other corridor along the river's entire length. As the battle rages between conservationists and developers, the riverbanks show scars from past battles or remain untouched because a battle was won or because a new one is waiting to be fought. Here, in microcosm, is the headlong growth now swallowing much of rural America and forever altering the American landscape.

We drifted past centuries-old farms with their homes perched on the highlands, past country clubs filled with million-dollar homes, under highway bridges that carry 200,000 motorists each day, and through national park property that provided glimpses of the river as it was just thirty years ago, before Atlanta spread beyond its original outer boundary.

Leaving behind the fisherman and a host of other anglers, we floated through the misty green landscape, past the abandoned iron girders of Settles Bridge and beneath the concrete and steel and motor traffic of Littles Ferry Bridge, with Fulton County on our starboard and Gwinnett on our port. In the early part of this century two Alpharetta thieves who'd just robbed a Suwanee bank made their getaway across the bridge that used to stand here. They sped into Fulton County, stopped, hopped out, and tossed the tim-

ber planks into the river, rendering the bridge impassable.

We camped that night at the mouth of Suwanee Creek. It was the last time we'd pitch our tent in north metropolitan Atlanta. Downstream, legal camping would be virtually impossible as the riverfront became increasingly filled with homes. Where land is protected, as in the Chattahoochee River National Recreation Area, camping is not permitted. For the remainder of our journey through the city, we stayed with our families, commuting to the river each day like office workers headed downtown.

A mile below Suwanee Creek stand the remains of Rogers Bridge, the last operating iron bridge between Buford Dam and Atlanta. The rickety old structure carried cars until the late 1970s. A mile up Rogers Bridge Road in Fulton County sits the century-old farmhouse and farm of John Taylor. The farm and the farmer reflect the same rugged character of the rusting bridge, and sadly, all seem bound to vanish into history. Progress is inevitable. Taylor's two daughters aren't farmers.

Taylor, approaching eighty, still runs cattle and cuts hay on his eighty-odd acres. He was raised by his maternal grandparents in the farmhouse. Before the turn of the century, Albert and Sarah Bell converted a long cotton storehouse on the property into a home, gathering rocks and red clay to construct the fireplace and chimney. The modest vinyl-sided home that their grandson occupies today incorporates a series of additions that surround the original structure. It sits by itself on the deadend road leading to the old bridge and commands a view of rolling pasture and ruminating cows. A weathered wooden sign out front bears the words "Riverside Farm—John and Polly Taylor."

If you travel a quarter mile in either direction from Riverside Farm, you run into rows of fine modern homes, lined up acre to acre in newly created subdivisions with names that attempt to create a sense of place on land that just years ago was nothing more than forest and farmland: The Homestead, Quail Hollow on the Chattahoochee, The Estates ($200,000 and more),

John Taylor at Riverside Farm

Glenwood at Sugar Mill (from $200,000).

"Most of the people that's around here now—well, a few of them come from Atlanta—but most of them are Yankees," Taylor told us. "They don't bother me or nothin' except that I just don't want them to build them damn houses here on top of me. I've seen enough of that here."

At the highest point on his property, Taylor looks east across the floodplain and the river into Gwinnett County, where a line of white apartment buildings interrupts the green horizon. "All the upland was in cotton; corn down in the bottoms, corn fifty cents a bushel, cotton five cents a pound," he said.

"I'd like to see the land stay just like it is.

Some folks might think that's selfish, but it isn't, if you love the land like I do."

Taylor is full of stories collected from a lifetime on the river.

Years ago there was an old boy named Johnny Scarrett that run a garage on the other side of The Varsity on Spring Street. He got interested in messing around with the river and came up here, and we got some people to build a boat for us. He brought a 1935 Ford engine up here and put that thing in there [in the boat]. Man, you talk about something that'd get on down the road—it would go!

He came up here one weekend and said, "Let's get the boat out and ride." We had it down in the barn on a little trailerlike thing. I said, "That river's just too low right now. There ain't enough water." "Aw," he said. "We'll make it."

We got it out down there and we decided to go downriver. We got down there just before you get to Abbotts Bridge, and he was really going on, and I was settin' up there, and all the sudden we hit a sandbar. I'll bet you I went 40 feet down the river. It unloaded all of us. The thing running as fast as it was, there was no way you could stay on it, you just had to go. Didn't hurt nobody to speak of—just scared us pretty bad.

Beyond the north Fulton farmland of the Taylor, Embry, and Moss families, we entered an area of megahomes. Atlanta Braves pitcher John Smoltz lives in an Atlanta Country Club home overlooking the river. His teammate, shortstop Jeff Blauser, was a regular trout hunter on this stretch of river before he left to play in Chicago. Millionaires here are as common as the kingfishers, and their homes are strikingly different than Taylor's place at Riverside Farm.

The cows have the run of the bottomlands at Riverside Farm. An old henhouse, a smokehouse, and a hay barn dot the pasture. On the pine-paneled walls of the Taylor home, the ubiquitous framed Osh Kosh clothing poster picturing two toddlers in overalls reads "You been farmin' long?" Near it is a print of the Mount Zion Methodist Church.

But just downriver, there are estates whose formal gardens are almost as expansive as Taylor's pastureland. Swimming pools and tennis courts cover backyards, not farm buildings. Inside, you'll find massive home entertainment centers, hot tubs, and commissioned works of art worth thousands of dollars hanging on the walls.

The disparate lifestyles of Taylor and the millionaires of north Fulton County within seven river miles was astounding but illustrative of the forces shaping our country's rural landscape and indicative of our society's accelerating patterns of consumption.

During the early 1990s, each day, an estimated 3,500 acres of the country's rural land was bulldozed for development. Between 1982 and 1992, Georgia lost 2 percent (some 740,000 acres) of its farm and forest land to development. If the landscape continues to change at that pace, warned one environmental organization in 1996, Georgia's land surface would be mostly covered by humanity in less than ninety years.

Viewing the upscale subdivisions, gated communities, and estates of north Fulton from our canoe, it was easy to see that the size of the average American home has grown steadily since World War II. Fueled by a consumer economy that remains healthy only if consumers are buying more and bigger goods, Americans' standard of living has spiraled beyond our grandparents' wildest dreams. Items once considered luxuries are increasingly being called necessities. In fact,

the U.S. Bureau of Labor Statistics added television sets to its cost of living index all the way back in 1951. In Atlanta's turn-of-the-century homes, the most common electrical appliance, excepting the light bulb, was the housewife's iron. Today, irons are an after-thought on wedding registers, and the average Atlanta home requires a web of electrical outlets for everything from computers to toothbrushes.

At Riverside Farm, John Taylor holds tightly to his land and has his property deeded to his children. He's refused more than a dozen land speculators over the years even though his property could easily fetch more than $3 million.

"They didn't offer anything. I wouldn't let them offer anything," he told us. "I just tell them I'm not interested—just pass it by and forget it. I don't want to be bothered with money. All I want's a good living and to take care of my children. I'm not interested in getting rich."

When he passes away, Taylor will be buried in the old Rogers-Bell Cemetery off Rogers Circle. The well-tended graveyard, surrounded by a whitewashed fence, sits on an acre between two new homes that list for more than $400,000. The development that Taylor has fought off for so many years will ultimately surround him in his final resting place.

"Progress is progress. It's good and it's bad and it's inevitable, I know," said twenty-nine-year-old Chris Scalley, a Chattahoochee trout-fishing guide who earns his keep taking doctors, lawyers, and other professionals on excursions between Atlanta and Buford Dam.

Scalley's business card shows the tail and head of a trout floating across the Atlanta skyline. Its surreal quality is in some ways appropriate. Atlanta's trout fishery on the Chattahoochee, the southernmost trout waters in the country, isn't real. It was artificially created by

Chris Scalley in the river near Jones Bridge

an ambitious state stocking program designed to exploit the clear, frigid fifty-degree water coming off the tailrace at Buford Dam.

The catfish that young men like John Taylor caught on cornbread and onion balls in the pre-dam days have fled downriver to warmer climes, leaving the river to trout and to anglers like Scalley. Scalley grew up on the river in Roswell and knows that he owes his livelihood and his love of trout in large part to Buford Dam.

"It was a natural thing to wind up on the river," Scalley told us. "The Hooch really got me going. This old fella used to always show up on the backwaters [of Bull Sluice Lake]. He had a fly rod with a bird dog that would sit at the front of his canoe. It looked cool! He was always catching *all* these fish, so one day I paddled over there and said, 'How in the world do you do that?' and he spent the day with me and gave me a box of flies. I was only twelve years old then, so I kind of fell into it."

Scalley is attuned to the spring caddis-fly

hatches, knows the stumps that hold rainbows, and pulls from the river spectacularly colored brown trout each fall. He also frets over progress that fills tributaries with sediment and turns the river the color of the state's famous red clay.

Like the aquatic insects that make up the trout's diet, Scalley is an "indicator species." His fate is tied to the bottom of the food chain. If tributaries become so silted that they can't support aquatic insects, if the river's spawning habitat is covered with dirt, if the caddis flies fail to hatch, Scalley's fishery will dry up.

"The local trout fisherman is an endangered species for sure," he said. "It's a great resource right now, and I know I've got to watch it. It's my future. But nature is so resilient, it's amazing what's still there. We catch a lot of fish inside the city limits, I'll tell you that."

Upstream from Scalley's childhood home in Roswell and just below Holcomb Bridge Road, we paddled by the curious stone pillars that once supported McAfee's Bridge. The pillars are remarkable in their resiliency, much like the river itself. In 1834 workers built the pillars by stacking large flat stones, one after another, until they reached the tops of the river's banks. No mortar was used, but the pillars have withstood floods and freezing for more than 160 years. Union troops reportedly burned the bridge in 1864, and it wasn't rebuilt until 1906 when the original Holcomb Bridge was constructed using the very same pillars. At the time of the Civil War it was the only bridge spanning the Chattahoochee apart from a railroad bridge near Bolton.

Around the bend sits Horseshoe Bend Golf Club, and here golf balls become as common as crawfish on the sandy river floor. Further downstream we hit the backwaters of Bull Sluice Lake, an impoundment formed in 1904 with the completion of Morgan Falls Dam, a hydro plant that powered Atlanta's streetcar system.

The sediment load created by the area's intense land development is most apparent on Bull Sluice. Branches of the lake that once held three and four feet of water can now barely float a small boat. Bends in the river that once permitted several vessels to pass at once now sometimes require boats to wait in line for their turn. If you step barefoot into the upper end of the lake where a strong river current persists, your toes will sink pleasantly into a dark brown sandy bottom. If you try the same thing at the bottom of the lake near the dam, you will sink knee deep in muddy muck. The heavier sand settles out quickly when the current slows, but the lightweight sediment holds out until the current virtually stops. Within 100 yards of the dam, the silt has created huge islands of cattails. During the year following our portage around the dam, the Georgia Power Company was forced to dredge in front of its intake structures in order to continue generating electricity.

Roger Buerki on the Diving Rock

Below the Morgan Falls Dam lies the river of my childhood, an eight-mile playground for rafters, fishermen, joggers, bikers, and hikers. In 1976, my family could rent a four-man raft outfitted with paddles and life jackets for $12.50. On any summer weekend, we could put it on the river and float all day along with a thousand or so others. It was, as Atlanta newspaper columnist Ron Hudspeth described it, "a people watcher's paradise. All kinds of humanity appeared: teenagers, tots, middle-aged, and even graybeards—everything from families to lonely people who hoped not to be so lonely by sundown."

The good times and the river's beauty spawned the Ramblin' Raft Race, a controversial annual rite of spring that attracted 300,000 in its heyday, filling the river with drunken, often naked, bodies and the detritus that came with them—beer bottles, cans, plastic chip bags, etc.

The politics surrounding the river at the time were equally entertaining and just as controversial. Without realizing it, Monica and I had planned our mountains-to-sea voyage for the twenty-fifth anniversary of the modern-day movement to protect the river from Atlanta's sprawl. The movement began in 1970 almost simultaneously in Washington, D.C., and Atlanta.

In Washington, officials with the Department of the Interior were busy drawing up a new concept for the parks system—urban national parks, and the Chattahoochee was one of the sites under consideration. At the same time in Atlanta, a Marietta resident named Roger Buerki stumbled upon an inconspicuous zoning notice tacked to a tree along the river at Rottenwood Creek in Cobb County. The county had a sewer line slated for the corridor, and that notice set Buerki's political feet in motion.

On the opposite bank, Fulton County had similar plans. A new riverfront office park and restaurant were under construction on the southeast corner of I-285 and the river. The new construction required sewer links, and the county's solution was to run a sewer trunk along the banks of the river through the cliffs at Palisades, including the Diving Rock, arguably the most scenic spot on the river's entire 436 miles. Engineers planned to blast a shelf out of the cliffs and set the pipe atop the level shelf for all to see. As one Fulton County official put it: "I don't see anything wrong with a sewer line, and no one uses the river except hippies anyway."

Buerki and others were appalled. These threats and callous attitudes of government officials galvanized a small but fiercely dedicated

group of individuals who called themselves "River Rats." The River Rats joined forces officially as the river protection group called Friends of the River. The next ten years saw the defeat of Fulton's ill-conceived sewer plan, the passage of the 1973 Metropolitan River Protection Act, and ultimately the creation of the Chattahoochee River National Recreation Area.

These were hard-fought victorics for the Friends as the political climate of the time was particularly hostile toward conservationists.

During a public hearing in Cobb County, Commissioner Ernest Barrett told Buerki: "Just because you want to save a tree doesn't mean we're going to change our plans. Sit down!"

Finally, during the debate over funding for the national recreation area, Larry McDonald, Buerki's congressman from Cobb County, called the multiunit park "bumps on a log that would provide refuge for hooligans, drug users and nudists."

Today, the recreation area encompasses 4,200 acres held in numerous tracts between Buford Dam and Peachtree Creek. It attracts more than 3 million visitors each year. It has cost taxpayers more than $80 million, but Atlantans cherish this haven in the midst of their urban landscape. Mothers pushing toddlers in strollers far outnumber the hooligans, and rafters still enjoy the unbridled freedom of a plunge from the Diving Rock. If you visit the park units often enough, you'll no doubt run into Buerki, still a River Rat. He'll be picking up trash or planting a native tree on land that he considers a kind of personal legacy.

Aside from that legacy of protected land, the River Rats' greatest triumph is probably the way they helped change the city's attitude toward the river. Their efforts made Atlantans take notice of the river. Until then most paid little attention to the river.

In 1951 the *Atlanta Journal* published an article about the river by Jack Spalding. He characterized the city's relationship with the river in the following words: "Atlantans generally regard their river as something jaundiced looking and full of rocks, mainly suitable for the production of catfish. It is not an impressive sight, but an impressive amount of water flows down its channel." In 1994, *Atlanta Journal-Constitution* columnist Colin Campbell wrote: "C'mon baby, lemme be your groupie, You're my pretty Chattahoochee. . . . Atlanta does have a great river—the beautiful (but raped) Chattahoochee."

Ironically, Buford Dam also contributed to the change in public perception of the river. With Buford Dam catching all of north Georgia's sediment and releasing clear cold water from its tailrace, the muddy brown river that Atlantans of the early 1900s had known was transformed into an inviting green current like a mountain stream. More than one Atlanta old-timer has told us how much prettier the river became after the completion of Buford Dam.

At Paces Ferry Road, the final jumping-off point before Peachtree Creek and the wastewater treatment plants dotting the river's shores in south Fulton and Cobb Counties, we beached our canoe to spend an evening at my parents' home nearby.

Students were walking home from Lovett School at the end of the day, and across the river from the school, the old Robinson's Restaurant complex was abuzz with construction. Outside we ran into Gerry Klaskala, who told us that he was opening a new restaurant there—a place called Canoe. It would be one of the city's only two restaurants sitting on the banks of the river. Construction of the other, currently Ray's on the

Gerry Klaskala at Canoe

River, had brought some of the River Rats' original protests in 1970.

"People like to be on the water, and there's no ocean in Atlanta. This is what we've got," Klaskala told us. "It's like a bonfire. People can sit and stare at a bonfire forever. The river's the same way. It's always flowing and changing. People are mesmerized by it."

Klaskala's Canoe opened that fall and quickly became one of Atlanta's hottest new restaurants. Undoubtedly, the peaceful, mesmerizing river contributed to its success.

Morning on Bull Sluice Lake near Willeo Creek, Fulton County

Morning near Abbotts Bridge, Gwinnett County

Morning fog at Rottenwood Creek, Cobb County

Clouds near Holcomb Bridge, Fulton County

Morning at Palisades, Fulton County

Cliffs at Palisades, Fulton County

Fall reflections at Thornton Shoals, Cobb County

Morning near Long Island Creek, Fulton County

Shoals at the mouth of Peachtree Creek, Fulton County

CHAPTER SIX

LIFE ON "DEAD RIVER"

WHERE PEACHTREE CREEK MEETS THE CHATTAHOOCHEE IN ATLANTA, THE RIVER changes. Opposite Peachtree's mouth, Cobb County's R. L. Sutton Wastewater Treatment Plant empties its effluent into the river. Around the bend and below the Atlanta Road bridge, Atlanta's R. M. Clayton Wastewater Treatment Plant does the same.

During our next thirty-five miles of paddling to the Fulton/Coweta county line, we saw outfall from twelve wastewater treatment facilities and the detritus discarded by a careless city. In a few short miles, the river had been transformed from Atlanta's playground into Atlanta's dumping ground.

The seventy-odd river miles between Peachtree Creek and Franklin at the head of West Point Lake in Heard County have evolved into the red-headed stepchild of the river—neglected, abused, forgotten, and described in all manner of derogatory terms: "Dead River," "devoid of life," "the great open sewer that is the Chattahoochee," "a nightmarish scene that might have been etched by Gustave Doré," "a septic tank."

No canoeing guidebook ever published directs you to a stream so described, but here we were, smack dab in the middle of the stench. Paddling the Chattahoochee through south Fulton, Cobb, and Douglas Counties, we discovered, was a lesson in what happens when you flush the toilet. Sewage is the least glamorous of all public policy issues, and elected officials and citizenry alike want to ignore it. We want our waste out of sight and mind. The same attitude permeates the Chattahoochee south of Atlanta. Few people travel or visit the river's industrialized corridor through south Fulton County (there is only one public boat ramp in the forty miles between Peachtree Creek and Whitesburg in Carroll County). To the extent that no one witnesses the tragedy, it remains out of mind. By averting our eyes we are able to pretend that the problem doesn't exist.

Even in wastewater management circles, jargon makes discussion less distasteful. What was once sludge is now biosolids. Sewage plants have become water reclamation facilities. Workers in these plants are pollution control engineers.

The story of Atlanta's sewers tracks the history of wastewater management from the dawn of water closets to the present and painfully reflects the folly of our collective denial. "Atlanta has woefully neglected her sewerage," reported the city's first committee on sewers and drains. The year was 1884, when Atlanta was still a privy town. At that time fourteen miles of sewer lines led from the few affluent homes with flush toilets to sidewalks, pastures, and creeks within 600 yards of the town's center. The city's first sewer was a ditch created by the spring that formed the main stem of the South River, which, in a public health nightmare, at the time also served as the city's primary water source. Around 1880, city workers lined it with rocks and covered it. Once it had been physically covered, the public began forgetting about it, establishing a tradition that persisted for the next 110 years.

By the end of the 1880s, the city's 2,829 flush toilets and 9,000 privies were creating a waste management dilemma. Twelve two-horse "night soil" wagons, or, as some called them, "honey wagons," serviced the city's privies. Each night workers dumped their load outside the city limits. In 1889, the wagons transported 7,112 loads of human excrement.

The following year, Atlanta put in place its first sewer system. Some of its original sewer lines are still in use today. The system, constructed under the direction of city engineer Robert Morris Clayton, carried waste outside the city in large trunk lines that emptied into five of the city's creeks. Engineers at the time believed that plentiful flowing water would purify the waste. Atlanta now had thirty-five miles of sewer lines and five contaminated creeks, some of which ran through the densely populated neighborhoods of former slaves, but the city's center smelled less objectionable.

For the next two decades, the city relied on this system, and as a result, typhoid death rates in Atlanta remained among the highest in the country, particularly among blacks. U.S. Census reports for 1905 show that typhoid deaths in Atlanta were more than double the national average. A 1908 study by the city's Chamber of Commerce titled "Urgent Needs of Atlanta" reported 16,295 water closets in use and 50,000 residents still relying on privies. The city's night soil carts still rolled out of town, and at the end of the sewer lines, the city's creeks labored with their smelly freight.

The city's geographic shortcomings as a major metropolitan area—in particular its lack of a large body of water, either river, lake, or ocean—compounded the city's sewer headaches as they necessitated the construction of Buford Dam in the 1950s to supply drinking water.

Larger cities like New York and Philadelphia dumped their untreated waste in major rivers like the Delaware and Hudson, where plentiful water diluted sewage and carried it to sea. Atlanta, having only tiny streams like Proctor and Peachtree available as repositories, was quickly forced to begin treating its sewage. During dry spells in 1908, up to 30 percent of Proctor's flow consisted of waste.

The crisis pushed Atlanta to the cutting edge of wastewater technology and made it one of the first American cities to adopt modern treatment methods—an ironic twist of history from today's perspective. By 1914, city workers under the direction of Clayton had installed Imhoff tanks, the forerunner of today's septic tanks, at the ends of the sewer lines on Entrenchment, Proctor, and Peachtree Creeks. The tanks were the first of their kind in the country, and Atlanta gained international attention for its progressive measures.

Once again, however, Atlantans quickly outgrew their sewer system. It took the Great Depression and the release of millions of dollars in federal funds to create the city's first true wastewater treatment plants. President Roosevelt's Work Projects Administration army constructed three treatment facilities in Atlanta, including the R. M. Clayton Plant on the banks of the Chattahoochee. The Clayton plant, completed in 1938 and named in honor of the man responsible for the construction of the city's original, inadequate sewer system, was designed to treat 42 million gallons daily and thereby to solve the city's wastewater woes.

The solution worked for a time, but growth never stopped. By 1951, 980 miles of sewer lines crisscrossed the city. During the decade, the city's population swelled to over 400,000. The river south of Atlanta, still frequented by fishermen some of whom earned their living from the river's catch, began to decline. Pollution, the city learned, was merely population spelled inside out.

By the mid-1960s, the Clayton plant was receiving twice its daily treatment capacity. Each day up to 50 million gallons of untreated sewage was diverted directly to the river. The same thing was happening across the state. In 1962, there were fifty-one Georgia municipalities that had no sewage treatment facilities.

In 1968 an expansion of Clayton that would triple its capacity was begun at a cost of $33 million. The city planned completion by 1971, but as so often happened in the city's wastewater management throughout the century, there were continual delays—first to 1972, then to 1973, then to 1974. The passage of the 1972 Clean Water Act ensured that the city would ultimately have to correct its problem, and the act released millions in federal assistance to finish the work. Nevertheless, upgrades weren't completed until 1978, and even then the plant was labeled the state's "largest water pollution problem." In 1971, when Rozelle and Kuniansky paddled the river's length, a cut on Rozelle's toe became so infected that it required medical attention. The doctor was quick to blame the river's foul water.

The massive daily dumping has long since stopped, and the river has improved noticeably, but Atlanta and the Clayton plant remain the river's biggest point source polluters. The city's growth has continued to outstrip expansion of the treatment plant, and more stringent treatment requirements mandated by the Clean Water Act have added to the difficulties of treating all the city's sewage. A matrix of 2,100 miles

Holly Elmendorf at Atlanta's R. M. Clayton Plant

of sewer lines now courses to the city's three main treatment plants. Though Clayton boasts a primary treatment capacity of 120 million gallons daily (making it the largest such facility in the Southeast), during the two years following our journey, the city reported sixteen major sewage spills of more than 10,000 gallons and fifty-four lesser spills.

Demonstrating today's increased environmental sensitivity, a story on a sewage spill of 800,000 gallons at the plant in 1997 made front-page headlines in the Atlanta newspapers. In 1970, the daily spills of 50 million gallons rarely received public notice.

Monica and I considered ourselves lucky. The river that lay ahead of us was far less noxious than the cesspool faced by Rozelle and Kuniansky. Our first stop was the Clayton plant, where we met Holly Elmendorf, an engineer working at the facility. A student at Duke Uni-

versity when the Clean Water Act became law, she was drawn into the environmental movement through the technological back door.

At the time, college students were donning gas masks and picketing with signs reading "Fight Dirty," while television showed an Indian shedding a tear at roadways littered with trash. Elmendorf responded by immersing herself in science.

"I wanted to save the world from water pollution, but I didn't want to be a radical environmentalist," she told us. "I wanted to do it from a technical approach and not from an advocacy approach." Engineering studies at Georgia Tech brought her to the Clayton plant in 1983, where she is a proctologist among engineers—a wastewater engineer.

During our tour of the Clayton plant, Elmendorf walked us past large cylindrical settling tanks filled with sewage. On the bottom of the tanks a mechanical arm scrapes solids into digesting tanks. Periodically, workers skim off the surface of the tanks any tampons and applicators that have slipped through the filters.

We viewed vats of bubbling sewage. Blowers aerate the sewage and oxygen-enriched, naturally occurring microorganisms further break down solids. Condoms, a wastewater engineer's nightmare, inflate on the surface of the cauldron, pumped by the aeration. Workers at the plant can gauge the city's sexual activity by the number of condoms that sneak through the plant's filtering system.

"I never knew they came in so many colors," Elmendorf said. "People just don't understand what happens when they flush the toilet."

We peered into the plant's red hot incinerators where biosolids are burned to ashes. The inert ashes, Elmendorf told us, are carried off by the Chattahoochee Brick Company, which incorporates them into its bricks. When we called the company to learn more about this remarkable recycling, a spokesman cautiously confirmed the story. He said it wasn't a processing detail that the company openly advertised. Still, the practice has obvious positive benefits: the ash would otherwise take up space in a landfill. In fact, the bricks helped build a legacy in the city's new Olympic stadium.

In the 1990s, the city was under intense pressure to clean up its wastewater act and was paying daily fines to the state for failing to treat its sewage properly. In 1995, the fines amounted to almost $4 million. Three years later, the total had ballooned to more than $20 million.

At the time of our visit, Elmendorf and other city engineers were reeling from the recent defeat—politically charged—of a major sewer project that in all likelihood would have eliminated the city's abuse of the river. The project was called "The Tunnel."

The Tunnel called for a channel eight miles long to be drilled 200 feet underground from the Clayton plant to the city's Utoy Creek treatment facility in southwest Atlanta. The massive subterranean canal, fashioned after a similar project in Chicago, would have put the city at the forefront of wastewater technology just as the Imhoff tanks had done in 1912. The city had just spent three years and $20 million completing the Tunnel's design. Officials hoped to have it operational by 1998, but before the city council could put the plan in action, race suddenly became a factor.

In February 1994, 100 angry black residents who lived near the Utoy Creek plant stormed a meeting of the utilities committee and demanded that the city drop the project. The residents branded the Tunnel "environmental racism" and claimed the city was attempting to pump the sewage of affluent whites into a predominantly black neighborhood. One elderly man at the meeting waved his cane and hollered at white council members, "Racist! Racist! Racist!" Activists distributed flyers warning neighborhood residents that the Tunnel would carry diseases to the black communities and would even increase residents' risk of cancer. The charges were wholly false.

When the measure came before the entire council in March 1994, 150 black residents packed the council chambers, and the council killed the project by a 12–6 vote that split almost entirely along racial lines. Newly elected Mayor Bill Campbell, who had voted in favor of the project as a council member, promised to veto the project if it got past the council. The city had wasted $20 million, and the alternative—expanding the Clayton plant—would cost $52 million more than the Tunnel plan. Elmendorf and other city engineers went back to the drawing table.

"To get to 100 percent design on the Tunnel project and then say, 'No, we're not going to do it that way'—It's very frustrating," Elmendorf said. "The designs that had been done seemed like a technically good solution."

We left the Clayton plant wondering where to place the blame for the outcome. Having grown up within noseshot of the Clayton plant, I couldn't blame black residents for opposing the plan. The city's first sewers had wreaked public health havoc in disenfranchised black neighborhoods, and it seemed fitting that this time a small, powerful black contingent had kicked the sewage back to north Atlanta and the racially mixed community surrounding the Clayton plant.

But by all scientific criteria, the Tunnel was the best plan for the entire city, the river, and the downstream communities. While a campaign of misinformation and emotions raged, Atlanta's leaders failed to educate their constituents. The leadership stood silent while unsubstantiated cries of racism obscured scientific considerations and ultimately the need to save the river. Siding with science was tantamount to supporting white Atlanta. No black leader wanted to be labeled an "Uncle Tom."

Below the Clayton plant, we paddled past black fishermen casting from the banks. They fished directly downstream of Clayton's pipes and at the mouth of Utoy Creek where the Utoy and Entrenchment Creek plants spill their effluent. While both blacks and whites frequent the national recreation area north of Peachtree Creek, downstream it's mostly a black man's river. Whites, particularly a young couple in a canoe, are unusual visitors. We got stares that

made us feel like Martians. The gulf between black and white seemed suddenly large and long.

We ran past Six Flags over Georgia, with its hulking rollercoasters reaching skyward above the river's north bank. We also passed sprawling flotillas of trash pinned against trees bending toward the water's surface. We saw basketballs, tennis balls, plastic oil jugs, Styrofoam coolers, plastic drink bottles, fire extinguishers, tires, whiskey bottles, condoms, children's toys, and almost anything else you could name. A dead opossum hung high in a tree over the water. A large, bloated pig rotted half submerged at the river's edge. The smell of treated effluent was ever present but not necessarily disgusting. Monica described it as "laundry water—a mix of chlorine, poop, and river dirt."

The riverfront homes that had been common in north Atlanta ceased altogether. The river's corridor in south Fulton, Cobb, and Douglas Counties has ironically been protected from development by Atlanta's pollution; no one wants to live on a smelly river. Green walls of sycamore, elder, sweet gum, cottonwood, ash, and river birch flank both sides, and the industrial parks, with few exceptions, sit beyond the river's viewshed.

As we headed into the sunset, following the river's westward course to Alabama, the riverside trees shook in the spring wind. Billowy white cottonwood seeds began drifting across the river like snow. The sun caught the seeds, backlighting them beautifully. It was a peaceful scene that seemed strangely out of place on this troubled stretch of water. It occurred to us then that the Chattahoochee was simultaneously a national park and an industrial park. If the smell didn't overwhelm us as we paddled through, the beauty surely would.

The city gave way to rural landscape, and

once again, camping spots became easy to find. One night we slept along a gas pipeline where, several hundred yards from the river, we found a deer stand, sitting about ten feet above the ground. A La-Z-Boy recliner sat inside the blind. Farther downstream, we camped at the mouth of the Dog River, a tributary that serves as Douglas County's water supply. At dusk we paddled into the Chattahoochee to watch the beavers. They were everywhere. We were finding this so called "Dead River" very much alive.

At the Georgia Route 16 bridge that leads to Newnan in Coweta County and to Whitesburg in Carroll County, we were greeted by fifth graders from Arnco-Sargent Elementary School. They held up a homemade sign that read "Arnco-Sargent Welcomes Joe & Monica." From the boat ramp, we traveled about two miles by bus to the Coweta County school, where principal Chris Jennings had gathered some 500 children on the front lawn. The children sang, "Row, row, row your boat gently down the stream, merrily, merrily, merrily, merrily, life is but a dream."

The welcome covered us with goose bumps. The song couldn't have been more appropriate as we played out a childhood dream. That day we talked to all the children, class by class. When we asked them how the river got its name, one kindergartner raised his hand and guessed, "From Alan Jackson's song 'Chattahoochee.'"

Jackson, the country music superstar, is a legend in his home county. His up-tempo tune about coming of age in rural Georgia made "Chattahoochee" a household name across the country. It was voted country music's top single of 1993 and became the twentieth-century equivalent of Sidney Lanier's "Song of the Chattahoochee."

Jackson and his contemporaries are among the sixth generation of Coweta and Heard coun-

tians to grow up swimming at Hilly Mill Creek near the Chattahoochee. The creek, which empties into the river just southwest of the Powers Crossroads, has a long history. A forty-foot waterfall about 200 yards from the creek's mouth was the site of a nineteenth-century grist mill. The pool at the base of the falls served as the baptismal for nearby Enon Grove Baptist Church. For most of this century, it has served as the area's top community outdoor recreation spot, and more residents than we could count told us they learned to swim in the cold deep hole. On Independence Day, hundreds would come to the spot, picnic baskets in one hand, fishing poles in the other, destined for the river side.

We paddled past Hilly Mill's falls, the smaller falls of Red Bone Creek within sight of the river, and through the islands at Bush Head Shoals, where hundreds of turtles poked their heads out of the water in the eddies behind each shoal. When we paddled over them they dashed under the surface and took cover in the rocks.

At Franklin, the first town we had seen since Helen that was truly on the river, we made camp in the city's ballpark beneath a canopy of water oak. The park was quiet except for walkers. While we cooked our pasta dinner, a big, blue Cadillac pulling an ugly brown boat came bouncing across the park's gravel road and stopped near our campsite. A short, spidery-looking fellow hopped out and began walking toward us.

"Uh-oh," we said. "We're in trouble now." No doubt we had violated some town law prohibiting camping in the park.

"Hi, I'm Gandy Glover," he said. "Sally Bethea, the riverkeeper, told me about y'all, and I had to come and meet you."

Relieved, for the next hour we ate dinner while Gandy spit his dip and entertained us with stories from the river. After the dishes were put

Gandy Glover with his Cadillac and dog cages

away, he carried us to the falls at Hilly Mill, where his family owns some 300 acres of river-front property. Thanks to Gandy, we had the chance to see the creek's famous falls for the first time by moonlight.

Propped up in the Cadillac's leather seats, we sped across the dirt roads of Heard County as if we had been in a Jeep. The boat and trailer bounced along behind us like tin cans tied to a newlyweds' car. Gandy's ride is probably the only Caddy in the state equipped with mudgrip tires. "Jeeps ride too rough," he said. The ugly boat behind us was a johnboat, powered by a state-of-the-art jet motor, all of which Gandy had painted Chattahoochee brown. "I took some mud to the paint store and said, 'Match that color,'" he told us. The camouflage was an attempt to make an expensive craft look less tempting to potential thieves.

Gandy, a fifth-generation native of Newnan, showed us photographs dating back to the 1920s. In one his grandfather sat with a crowd of bathers in the falls at Hilly Mill. Gandy's roots

here run as deep as his love for the river and the land. He is the type good ole' boy who, at all times, has within arm's reach a dip, a drink, a rifle, or a fishing pole. He's also one of Coweta's most successful real estate agents and served as the mayor of Newnan for eight years. When he lost his bid for a third term in 1993, the *Newnan Times-Herald* asked him about his plans. He said, "I'm going hunting in the morning."

During his first campaign in 1985, he made only two campaign promises: to get rid of an annoying stop sign on a main thoroughfare and to eliminate the pigeons downtown.

"People would come out of church and they'd crap on their new clothes," he said. "People were begging me to get rid of the pigeons. Somebody was going to charge the city $25,000 to put out poison corn.

"When I took office there were 1,200 pigeons downtown, 850 of which I killed the first year. I went under bridges, into attics. I'd crawl around up in all that nasty stuff and fire away—beebee guns, pellet guns, .22s, whatever it took."

Ask any Newnanite about Gandy Glover; they grin that telling grin and say, "He's a character."

Gandy took us back to our camp in the Cadillac, where we'd arranged a meeting the next day with Glover's hunting and fishing mentor, Junior Arrington, a native of Franklin and a Chattahoochee legend.

"I'd heard about him growing up," Glover said. "As soon as I got my driver's license, I went to Franklin and hunted him out. He taught me how to bow hunt and how to fish the river."

The two men have been friends ever since.

Arrington is a round, solid man with the build of a bulldog and a deep laugh. He drives an old Jeep that lists permanently to the driver's side under the weight of his tremendous frame. He and Susie, his wife, live in a home almost within casting distance of the river. Susie works, and Arrington, a retired electrician, hunts and fishes. Nobody knows the river in the area better. When someone turns up missing on the river, Heard County authorities give him a call.

"I know every rock—every deep hole on this river," he boasts. He has pulled more than a few bodies from its muddy water.

Arrington's grandfather, Frank Abner, earned part of his keep hauling catfish from the river along with other Franklin fishermen like Holt Pike and Bradley Johnson. Arrington grew up in the 1940s and 1950s, working his grandfather's cages and lines and tagging along to the river's fish camps at places like Bush Head Shoals. The camps were as much social clubs as fishing spots. Some held pool tables, jukeboxes, slot machines, and other forms of entertainment unrelated to fish.

"We had to make a living on the river because we farmed. By the time you farmed all year long, when you settled up from what you bought—fertilizer and all that stuff, you didn't make but 50 or 100 dollars," Arrington said.

Junior Arrington

If you didn't make something on the side, you just didn't have it. We sold catfish to cafés in Hogansville and LaGrange and everywhere else for ten cents a pound. And we trapped—muskrats, coons, mink, fox.

We trapped 'em, skinned 'em and stretched 'em on boards until they dried, and along about a month before Christmas, we'd send 'em to Sears Roebuck and they'd send a check back, and that's what we'd have Christmas with. Sometimes we'd get four or five hundred dollars.

We fished up until it got so polluted you couldn't do nothing with it. This river, I tell ya, it's in a lot better shape than it was twenty years ago. It got to where one time you couldn't hardly stay around it. It stunk.

The demise of Arrington's fishing grounds converted him into an atypical modern-day environmentalist in a country boy's clothing. We learned of him from Sally Bethea. He showed up at one of Bethea's early visits to Heard County

Sally Bethea, Riverkeeper

and hollered from the back of the room, "Where's this riverkeeper lady?"

One look and you know that Arrington's no sport-utility-driving Gortex-wearing granola eater. For a time, he trained as a professional wrestler, but he dropped the idea when he realized he didn't have the temperament to fake a fight. "I'd get too mad," he said.

"I was sitting up at the shoals fishing, and there was four people pulled up against the shoals drinking beer bottles, and—bam!—throwing 'em against the rocks," he said.

I said, "Hey, don't y'all do that no more. What if a young 'un come up here and jumped out and cut off a leg? I wade around in this thing too."

One of 'em said, "Ain't no business of yours!"

And I said, "Well I'm about to make it some of mine." I ran that big ole bass boat as close as I could get, and I just jumped out and waded over to where they's at. I told 'em, "I'll turn this boat bottom side up! I better not catch y'all up here doing something like that."

Bethea, an urban Gortex-wearing sport-utility driver, has spoken strongly about the fate of Arrington's fishing grounds. Her organization's lawsuits ultimately forced Atlanta to clean up its act. She has written that "the river south of Atlanta can and will be restored. Sewage treatment is not rocket science. The technology is available. It's just a matter of making sewage a priority."

And making sewage a priority will be a job for everybody—the urban advocates like Bethea, the rural sportsmen like Arrington, and the scientists and engineers like Elmendorf at the Clayton plant. There is no longer room for our out-of-sight, out-of-mind attitudes when it comes to wastewater. As Elmendorf told us, "Historically you just put your waste downstream away from you. Now everybody's downstream."

Morning at the mouth of Snake Creek, Cobb County

Moon at sunset in McIntosh Reserve, Carroll County

River cane and morning mist near Red Bone Creek, Heard County

Afternoon near White Oak Creek, Fulton County

Morning at McIntosh Reserve, Carroll County

Maple leaves at Bush Head Shoals Islands, Heard County

Falls at Hilly Mill Creek, Heard County

Morning on Acorn Bluff, Carroll County

Morning below Acorn Bluff, Carroll County

Morning on Bibb City Pond, Muscogee County

CHAPTER SEVEN

WATER OVER THE DAMS

BELOW FRANKLIN, WEST POINT LAKE AWAITED US WITH ITS 26,000 ACRES of flat water and thirty miles of hard paddling. The river's second major transformation behind a Corps of Engineers dam meant wind, motorboat wakes, and a long portage at the end of the lake.

We began to envision ourselves as the burly, bronzed paddlers in the opening credits of the old television series *Hawaii Five-O* who powered their outrigger across the South Pacific surf. We could hum the familiar theme song even if we could not paddle with the skill of the Hawaiian natives.

The upper end of West Point Lake is the catch basin for Atlanta's detritus. Where the river stops flowing, the natural cleansing motion also ceases. Trash falls out of the flow along with suspended nutrients carried from an urban watershed. The litter creates a visual nightmare and navigational hazards for motorboats.

At a sharp bend in the river near Fish Creek, we paddled through a brown scum. Tires, bottles, and cans floated in midstream. Water quality experts and environmentalists had warned of such scenes back in the 1960s when West Point Dam was first proposed. Unless the dam project was delayed until metropolitan Atlanta cleaned up its sewage, they said, the lake would be an algae-infested cesspool. The dam project was not delayed, but upgrades to Atlanta's treatment facilities have continually been delayed. The lake has suffered.

Eutrophication, the natural aging process experienced by all lakes in which mineral and organic nutrients accumulate, reduces dissolved oxygen and promotes aquatic plant life at the expense of animal life. This process has come early to West Point. In an impoundment of its size, eutrophication might normally take a century or more, but scientists were finding eutrophic conditions as early as the lake's thirteenth birthday in 1988.

Much to the dismay of business leaders in West Point and LaGrange, publicity stemming from the warnings about eutrophication and potential fish kills has spoiled the lake's reputation. Ironically, the Corps' first project in the Southeast to include recreation as a primary objective is now perhaps the most underused impoundment on the river. Some parks dotting the lake's shores are unkempt, unused, or altogether abandoned. We went ashore at one to find it closed. It had apparently not been touched for years. Weeds grew through the asphalt of the access road. Restroom doors and windows were shattered and rusting.

Yet at the very bend where we saw the brown scum and trash on the water's surface, we paddled beneath a sturdy pine where a bald eagle perched. We slid quietly beneath the bird, firing off a few shots with the telephoto lens before it became annoyed and lit out across the lake. The national park/industrial park dichotomy had now become habitual.

At Pyne Road Park we made camp and ventured into LaGrange, a quiet textile town that since the lake's impoundment in the early 1970s

has counted the water-oriented recreation industry among its economic calling cards. The trip to town, past LaGrange College and around Lafayette Square, was uneventful until we began hitchhiking back to the lake. Motorists on Georgia Route 109 ignored our thumbs, and we walked to the edge of town before a man in a pickup pulled over. When we asked for a ride to the lake, he told us to hop in, saying, "Aw, heck, I'll give you a ride. I ain't doing nothing but driving around getting drunk anyway." Already in the cab and desperate for transportation, we shrugged our shoulders and hoped for the best. He was a textile worker at a local mill enjoying a day off. Whether or not he was drinking, we reached our vessel safely.

Most people in LaGrange or West Point will say that the lake isn't nearly as polluted as people think. They'll tell you that West Point has a "perception problem" as much as a pollution problem.

The lake's bad public relations began in October 1988 when the Sunday *Atlanta Journal-Constitution* carried the front-page headline "Death by Pollution—Atlanta's Wastes Choking the Life Out of West Point Lake." The story's author, the longtime environmental reporter Charles Seabrook, immediately became something of a pariah in Troup and Heard Counties.

"Everybody hated Charles Seabrook at first," said Tommy Mike, a West Point fishing guide. "But it's turned out he's kind of a pioneer. That hurt, and it still lingers, but it was good that it came out when it did."

Probably no one has written more extensively about the Chattahoochee than Seabrook. His desk in the *Atlanta Journal-Constitution* newsroom is stacked so high with resource material on various environmental subjects that the

Charles Seabrook and Mount Seabrook at the *Atlanta Journal-Constitution*

chaotic mix of papers has become known among coworkers as Mount Seabrook. Information on the Chattahoochee forms the bedrock of the mountain.

Seabrook remembers the West Point story well. "That Monday my phone rang off the hook," said the bespectacled and balding reporter. "They were after my backside. They wanted to rip my lungs out. The fact that my story caused a near riot and a near lynching of me means I got my message across."

The story, based on studies conducted by Auburn University scientists, warned of impending fish kills caused by the hypergrowth of algae fertilized by the 3 million pounds of phosphorus and 13 million pounds of nitrogen that were pouring into the lake each year. The article shocked business owners dependent upon the recreation-based economy, who until then had

prospered from the lake's reputation as an excellent fishery. Local marinas and bait and tackle shops saw business drop up to 25 percent in the months following the article. News of a sewage spill of 400 million gallons at Atlanta's Clayton plant earlier in that year further tainted West Point's reputation, as did later reports of fish contaminated with toxic chemicals.

Still, the front-page news produced results. The following year, phosphorus detergent was banned in metropolitan Atlanta, and the state Department of Natural Resources (DNR) stepped up pressure on metropolitan treatment plants to reduce phosphorus discharges in effluent. Lake dependents demanded changes, angrily pointing fingers at their upstream neighbors. By 1993, the DNR was reporting 70 percent phosphorus reductions in treated effluent. The massive fish kills that had been predicted never materialized.

Though effects of the pollution persist, both real and perceived, and though we found some lake facilities abandoned or unused, things seemed to be on the rebound in places during our traverse of the lake. We ran into as much boat traffic as we had encountered on Lanier, and fishermen were everywhere. At Amity Park, we camped next to a spit of land jutting into the lake that was filled with recreational vehicles and campers whose Christmas-colored lights, lanterns, bug zappers, and citronella candles created a carnivallike atmosphere under the full moon that rose above the pines at dusk. Everything seemed as it should be on the Saturday night before Mother's Day in west Georgia.

The following morning, Margaret Zachry, the downtown development coordinator for the town of West Point, carried us to Mother's Day services at the West Point First United Methodist Church. We walked into the sanctuary in our Sunday best—our least dirty T-shirts, shorts, and water sandals—and turned a few heads.

West Point, a tiny textile town that serves as the central business district for the outlying mill villages of Lanett, Shawmut, Riverview, and Langdale, straddles the Alabama/Georgia state line. The smaller Alabama villages set their clocks according to Georgia time. The area grew up around the textile industry, and the mills and company-built mill homes still dominate the landscape.

Downtown West Point sits squarely in the floodplain just three miles downstream from the dam, which rises ninety-seven feet from the riverbed and stretches the length of twenty-four football fields. Enough concrete was used in building the powerhouse to construct a sidewalk stretching from Atlanta to San Diego, boasts the

Corps literature. There is, perhaps, as much concrete in the dam as there is in all of West Point, but this small town is the reason for the dam's existence.

Before the dam plugged the river, West Point was periodically ravaged by floods. The Chattahoochee spilled into the town in 1886, 1901, 1912, 1916, 1919, 1929, and 1961. Early settlers, unlike the Creek Indians they displaced, unwittingly, perhaps defiantly, built their homes and businesses within the floodplain. They adapted by putting their outbuildings on stilts and raising the sidewalks in their business districts high above the streets. When the freshets came, merchants carried what goods they could to the second story, and likewise residents rolled up their carpets and headed upstairs.

The 1919 flood, West Point's worst, set in motion the town's movers and shakers, who believed an upstream dam could be their salvation. For J. Smith Lanier, the founder of the local telephone company and also the official town weatherman and flood crier, the dam became a lifelong pursuit. He left no political stone unturned, courting senators, representatives, business leaders, and even New York governor Franklin D. Roosevelt, who was already frequenting nearby Warm Springs. At one point, Lanier determined that the most successful lobbyists in Washington wore impressive beards, so he grew a handsome Vandyke of his own. He beat the drum incessantly.

A poem published in the *West Point News* in the late 1920s was, no doubt, a result of his influence, if not of his hand:

It seems the Chattahoochee
Should have a harness put on her

When she dances the Hoochee Koochee
For she don't look very good, no sir. . . .

We will admit that she hath her charms,
When she's in her bed and still.
But not so, when she spreads her arms,
And they reach from hill to hill.

They say that we can build a dam,
Putting a stop to her depredations.
If we get consent of Uncle Sam
And he's the strongest of all nations.

Now, all the way from old Habersham,
And all the way down to the ocean,
People see a need of this dam,
So we make the following motion:

This river to be forever barred,
From scattering her mud and slime,
In everybody's house and yard,
From now 'til the end of time.

Now without a thought of temerity,
Let's speak right out to Uncle Sam,
And say to him in all sincerity,
Don't you think we're worth a dam!

Lanier's early courting of Roosevelt paid off in 1935 when the president approved a $595,000 project to widen and clear the river at West Point and construct a levee. The improved flood control also eliminated the town's Avenue A. Today the first road running parallel to the river's east bank is Avenue B, but despite the loss of a thoroughfare, grateful citizens presented Lanier with a silver tea service.

The levee proved only a temporary remedy.

Another catastrophic flood was needed to convince Congress that West Point was worth a dam. In March 1961, the river flowed into the city again. Boys of high school and college age, including Griggs Zachry, whom we met at his downtown boat dealership, donned wet suits and skied down Main Street. The wakes created by the rowdy teens were blamed for broken storefront windows, but to this day Zachry attributes the damage to the National Guard's mammoth amphibious vehicles that came down Main Street.

The following year, Congress passed the Flood Control Act, essentially authorizing the construction of West Point Dam. Groundbreaking ceremonies took place April 16, 1966, the 101st anniversary of the Civil War battle in which Union troops captured West Point. At the ceremonies, one old-timer remarked, "Maybe the Yankees are paying us back for all they tore up that day."

The dam was completed in 1975. It cost taxpayers $132 million to build and another $3 million to maintain each year. Ironically, the Corps' interpretive displays at the lake visitor center extol the virtues of floods as they benefited the Creek Indian farmers, replenishing the soil of the floodplain fields. More than one West Pointer told us that it would have been far cheaper to move the town of 3,000 than to build the enormous dam.

After portaging around the dam and paddling past Hames Island, a historic ford before the first bridges to West Point were built, we met Steve Johnson, a science teacher at Springwood School, an integration-era private school across the state line in Lanett. After we talked to his students about the river, he invited us to stay at his week-

Steve Johnson and his lilies on Flat Shoal Creek

sediment-free water remain. Before the construction of the river's numerous fall line dams, the lilies were likely abundant on the river's shoals.

Johnson, who has willed his Flat Shoal property to the Nature Conservancy, speaks with the reserved, dry drawl typical of a man reared in an old southern family. The last of his clan, he lives alone in his great-grandparents' home built in 1876. He represents the fourth generation of his family to occupy the home. The son of Aldine Johnson, who operated a sporting goods store in West Point from 1946 to 1972, he grew up reluctantly tagging along on his father's twice weekly fishing trips to the river.

"He sold mostly fishing tackle. At least that's what he wanted to sell, because fishing was his whole life. He went fishing every Wednesday and Sunday of his life," Johnson told us. "It seemed like I went fairly often, and I never really liked it. I enjoyed being outdoors, but I didn't like sitting still for so long. We'd stay out in the river until dark. We could never leave until it got dark."

Contradicting the sentiments of most West Pointers, the younger Johnson quietly opposed the dam. "I had been down the river in a canoe by that time, and I just liked the river the way it was. I didn't want to see it dammed up. Of course, I was the only one who didn't. Everybody around here just accepted it as something we just had to have."

Through the years Johnson has developed a love-hate relationship with his hometown, one that plays out similarly in small towns across the South. Though he has been a president of the historical society, a trustee at First Methodist, and a member of two library boards, he often yearns for more than his hometown has to offer. It has been that way since his childhood in the

end cabin on ancestral property bordering Flat Shoal Creek in Harris County, where colonies of rare spider lilies were just beginning to bloom.

The garden of lilies on Flat Shoal gave us a glimpse of the Chattahoochee as it might have looked in the early 1800s when Johnson's great-great-grandfather, Benjamin Johnson, settled in the area. The threatened lilies survive in the wild only along the fall line in Alabama, Georgia, and South Carolina where rocky shoals and flowing,

1950s when one of his complaints of small-town living was the lack of a foreign-language class at his high school. That complete education had to wait until he escaped to enroll at Emory University in Atlanta. If he were someone else—if his ties to family, history, and land not so strong—he might have stayed in Atlanta permanently. Instead he remains steadfastly and proudly a West Point Johnson—emotionally bound to his home. "Sometimes I envy people who don't have any roots. They can live anywhere they want to. But this is home to me, and it will always be home to me," he said, resigned to his long taproot in the floodplain.

In the thirty-five river miles between West Point and Columbus where the piedmont meets the coastal plain, eight dams clog the river—Langdale, Crow Hop and Riverview, Bartletts Ferry, Goat Rock, Oliver, North Highlands, City Mills, and Eagle-Phenix. In these thirty-five miles the river drops more than 300 feet in elevation. The geography attracted early settlers (and later industrialists) intent on harnessing the water's power, and the dams sprang up like the sycamores and river birch on the river's banks. Don Otey and Bob Sehlinger in *Southern Georgia Canoeing* said of this section: "slackwater, dull scenery and an abundance of portages combine to make this a paddle trip suitable only for bad dreams."

We remained determined to travel the river's length without motorized assistance, but as we left the boat ramp at the fire station in West Point, Zachry's words echoed through our heads: "People die down here on the river."

All but two of the dams ahead of us were open spillways. If we came too close to the lip, we'd be sucked over the edge, where the churning falls would pin us against the backside of the

dam and drown us. The Georgia Power Company had placed warning buoys in front of each spillway because two canoeists had died several years earlier.

At Langdale, we found a well-worn path on the Georgia side and began our carry. By the time we reached the bottom of the dam, the water level had jumped dramatically. West Point Dam eight miles upstream had begun its daily release. The unimpressive trickle that spilled over the dam when we began the portage was now a roaring torrent that looked like Niagara Falls.

We gingerly pushed off below the dam and maneuvered through the whitewater until the river began slowing again above Crow Hop. The river here is a maze of islands, and though we had a good map, it was hard to tell which channel would place us at the best portage. From our earlier scouting, we knew the far west channel would take us around an island to Riverview Dam, which appeared impassable on either bank. Crow Hop, Riverview's companion dam, lay somewhere in the middle of this maze. We didn't want to turn a corner and find ourselves on its lip in the rapidly rising river.

Ultimately, we found Crow Hop and a portage path, but the uncertainty made for some of the trip's tensest moments. Fishermen crowded the shoals below the Crow Hop spillway, casting for hybrid bass. We paddled between them, getting caught in a swirling rapid that turned our canoe sideways to the current and then spit us out straight downstream. The river and the Corps of Engineers seemed suddenly in control of our vessel.

At the boat ramp at Riverview, we ran into a crowd of locals fishing and drinking beer on the banks in the late afternoon shadows cast by the textile mill.

Morris Jackson at Goat Rock Dam

"I love this river," said one woman, a lifelong resident of the mill town. "But I'm afraid of it. It's dangerous anytime. I've got a lot of respect for it."

We couldn't have agreed more. As we shoved off, her husband yelled to her from their truck, "Come on, woman, they ain't from Riverview, they can't understand you."

Lake Harding and Bartletts Ferry Dam were our next stop. Impounded in 1926 and managed by the Georgia Power Company, the 5,850-acre reservoir has become known as Georgia's Little Mud Puddle. Modest cabins and cottages flank its shores. On one well-manicured island, a cottage sits among grape arbors, a gazebo, and banks of blooming hydrangea. Such quaint and secluded retreats are unheard of on most U.S. Army Corps of Engineers–managed lakes, where strict building codes and riparian setbacks are enforced. Elsewhere we ran into a pair of bare-chested men bow fishing. They trolled along the

shores in their boat, poised, arms cocked, arrows ready, focused on the underwater world like modern-day Creek hunters.

With the help of W. E. Pitts, who manages the Georgia Power Company's six fall line dams, we picked a portage route around Bartletts Ferry—across the dam and down the steep steps on the backside, where we had to turn the canoe sideways to squeeze it through the dam's narrow archways. At its base we took a right turn through the powerhouse, which vibrated and roared as the river whipped its six turbines into electric productivity.

Five miles downstream at Goat Rock Dam, Morris Jackson, Georgia Power's maintenance foreman, met us in his pickup and explained the half-mile portage. We let the pickup tote our camping equipment, but I crawled under the carrying yoke and walked the canoe around the dam while Monica shot photos.

Jackson and other workers had just removed

one of the dam's mammoth turbines for repairs. It sat outside the powerhouse, where we could see holes left by seven missing steel blades that had been spat out in the dam's tailrace during a noisy explosion. The propellerlike wheel that catches the falling water and turns the turbine was a shell of its former self after some eighty years of daily encounters with pressurized water aimed seaward. The turbines must be repaired frequently. Welders usually crawl into the penstocks to make minor repairs and reinforcement. In the dam's guts, only an eighteen-inch-thick gate of steel separates the workers from several thousand acres of water.

Jackson showed us around the powerhouse, taking us to his favorite spot—a narrow window that provides a spectacular view of the dam's sixty-eight-foot-high spillway. We had to shout over the roar.

"Sometimes I just have to go there and open the window and look out over the dam," Jackson said. "You need that time to let your conscience talk to you. A lot of times I find myself at that window. It brings you back down—It's a soothing thing."

Jackson, who grew up in the tiny Alabama community of Wacoochee Valley, about six miles west of Goat Rock, recalled seeing the spillway for the first time as a teenager.

"When I saw the outside of Goat Rock, it really shocked me," he said. "I didn't know anything this close to me was this big. And it's right behind the woods where I lived. I was fishing with my mother and I said, 'What is that?' and she said, 'That's Goat Rock. You're daddy worked there and your granddaddy worked there.'"

A few years after this first encounter and shortly after graduating from high school, Jackson began work at the hydro plant that Amos Jackson, his grandfather, had labored to build in 1912.

"I did everything from cutting grass to cleaning commodes," he said. "In the sixties, there was no advancement for black employees. The future was sort of dim, but the pay was a little more than what I was making."

A year later, the army drafted him and sent him to Vietnam with the 101st Airborne. Suddenly, the fifth of seven children born to Marvin and Effie Jackson in a segregated South saw a world larger than Goat Rock Dam.

"I thought it was terrible to be a black person in the United States in the sixties, but I got to Vietnam and I found out life wasn't so bad after all.

"I liked the service. It was more integrated at the time. It was different than being in Alabama. In the service everybody was treated basically the same."

He returned to the States determined to rise above utility worker status, but when he came back to Goat Rock, they gave him a lawnmower and commode brush.

Slowly he worked his way through the ranks. Lawsuits filed by black workers to address fairness in hiring broke down corporate color barriers, and Jackson bounced from plant to plant through the 1970s and 1980s. He went from McDonough, Wansley, and Yates to Atkinson and finally back home to the Chattahoochee, where, after training in technical school and earning an associate's degree at a local community college, he finally became a maintenance foreman and supervisor.

"Some black people make better managers simply because they've done swept the floor, they've done picked up cigarettes, and they've done cleaned commodes," he told us.

I've been through it, and I've come through the ranks. My mama told me, "If you forget where you came from, you don't know where you're going." That's the way I feel about things.

Even though things weren't what I thought they should have been back in the sixties, I'm grateful to be working for this company. It's educated my children and given me a livelihood and security. If it wasn't for these dams up and down the river, I could have been in a cotton mill down in Columbus, and God knows, I'm thankful for that.

Like the Jackson family, the communities along the fall line are closely linked to the dams. During the Civil War, Columbus was second only to Richmond as the South's leading industrial complex. Even though much of the town was ransacked in the closing days of the war, by 1878, Eagle and Phenix Mills had grown into the largest cotton and woolen mill in the South. The city's early dams made it all possible. By the early 1900s, Columbus was advertising itself as the "Electric City." The dams were lighting homes, propelling streetcars, and, most important, powering the textile mills stretched along the river between Columbus and West Point. The early twentieth-century dams were an economic boon for the area.

Today, the dams are relics of early twentieth-century engineering, rendered almost obsolete by the ever-growing demands of a burgeoning population. While the dams once lit the entire region, today their electricity couldn't power Columbus alone. Georgia Power, which operates twenty hydropower plants on Georgia rivers and supplies power to 97 percent of the state, gets only 3 percent of its electricity from hydro plants. The old dams simply can't match the output of fossil fuel and nuclear plants.

On our final night north of Columbus and the coastal plain, we camped on a knoll at the western end of Oliver Dam. The site provided the quintessential view of a dam—vast expanses of water on one side and bleak, abandoned, dry riverbed on the other. A wild river had been sacrificed in the name of progress. From this viewpoint, we were reminded that dams subjugate nature like nothing else. They break its reckless abandon and pump it through neatly arranged pipes. Unfortunately, rivers riddled with concrete, steel, and men wearing hard hats can be found in every corner of the country. Nationwide, 600,000 miles of rivers lie still behind 68,000 large dams. The Yellowstone River in Wyoming and Montana is currently the only major American river that remains undammed.

Below Oliver, the Chattahoochee drops an incredible 125 feet in elevation in less than three miles, a descent rivaling whitewater destinations like the Ocoee and Nantahala. But from the top of Oliver Dam, we found such wildness hard to imagine. Oliver and three other dams interrupt the natural fall. The following day we spent a full nine hours paddling, carrying, and lining our canoe through this short stretch of river. Before the dams were built, a Creek Indian in a dugout canoe could have blasted through the whitewater run in less than an hour.

In the pre-Olympic fervor that swept Georgia after Atlanta secured the 1996 Summer Games, a few river lovers from Columbus advocated breaching and removing several of the city's historic downtown dams to create a whitewater run and court the Games' canoe and kayak competition. Though no one living has ever seen the river in its unaltered state, historic accounts and present-day clues indicate that such a project would yield a thrilling ride, including possible Class IV and V rapids. The proposal never really

Neal Wickham at City Mills Dam

got off the ground, however. Columbusites are sentimental about the old dams and mill buildings, and returning the river to a seminatural state seemed entirely unnatural.

Neal Wickham, the longtime owner of a Columbus outdoor and sporting goods store, was still excited about the idea when we paddled into his town. "You'd have the best whitewater run within a metro area in the world right here in Columbus," he told us. "You might have to re-move a few truck bodies, a few refrigerators, and maybe a few bones, but you'd have a wonderful whitewater run."

Below Eagle-Phenix Dam, we pulled out at the site of Columbus's historic steamboat landing. In the first two months of our journey we had carried around twelve dams and cursed every one of them. Now we could celebrate. The three dams that remained came equipped with navigational locks.

Lower falls on Mulberry Creek, Harris County

Sunburst on West Point Lake, Troup County

Spider lilies on Flat Shoal Creek, Harris County

CLOCKWISE FROM TOP LEFT: *Trout lily, Cobb County; Wild ginger, Cobb County;*
Calypso flower, Liberty County; Atamasco lily, Gadsden County

Spring growth at Oxbow Meadows, Muscogee County

Spring growth at Riverview, Chambers County

Morning at Long Island Shoals, Fulton County

CHAPTER EIGHT

PICKING ON ALABAMA

DOWNRIVER FROM COLUMBUS ON THE BACKWATERS OF LAKE WALTER F. George (known as Lake Eufaula on the Alabama side of the river), we ran into Floyd McNeese and his son-in-law, Mitch Southall, poking along in their johnboat beneath a steep, wooded bank. Breambusters (glorified cane poles) in hand, they were pulling bream out of the river as quickly as they could bait their hooks.

We paddled alongside to say hello, shoot photos, and ask the question we'd been asking nearly everyone along this brown strip of water that forms the geopolitical boundary between Georgia and Alabama: "Why do folks from Georgia poke fun at their Alabama neighbors?" From West Point, where the river begins forming the state line, all the way to Lake Seminole, this question elicited more telling grins than any other. Nearly everyone had a comment and a joke.

McNeese, who lives on the Georgia side, immediately produced a rib-tickling Alabama joke. Meanwhile, Southall, the tolerant son-in-law and Alabama native, grinned and shook his head. He'd grown accustomed to the good-natured ribbing of his father-in-law.

I'm not sure when I heard my first Alabama joke. At a family reunion? At a University of Georgia football game? All I know is that these jokes are a part of me as a native Georgian. I think when they delivered babies like Monica and me at Piedmont Hospital in Atlanta they didn't slap our bottoms upon entering this world but simply told us an Alabama knee-slapper.

"Did you know the toothbrush was invented in Alabama?" the doctor might have asked rhetorically. "Otherwise, it would have been called a teethbrush." At these words, we toothless babies let out cries of delight.

If you are Georgian, you laugh at Alabama. Georgia's proudest, most brazen native sons and daughters will tell you they consider themselves intellectually, culturally, and economically superior to their neighbors to the west. The popular thinking among Georgians, regardless of evidence to the contrary, is that Alabamians are uneducated, uncultured inbreeds who live in mobile homes.

I've always assumed that the tradition had to do mostly with college football rivalries. My father's favorite Alabama joke is a true tale involving the gridiron. On the way to a football game one fall afternoon, he saw a roadside sign that read "R-O-L-E Tide." Georgia fans, though we'd like to think them better educated, nevertheless have it easier. "Go" is virtually impossible to misspell and "D-A-W-G-S" is accepted spelling around Athens.

My home state's superiority complex and its intense rivalry with Alabama have always perplexed me. We're not *really* so different from folks in Alabama, are we? On this journey along the state line, I thought Monica and I could find some answers.

Our search for truth began in earnest in Columbus, where we put the question to Fred Fussell, a folklorist with the Historic Chattahoochee Commission, an organization that promotes tourism and historic preservation through-

out the Chattahoochee Valley (on both sides of the river). We thought Fred might have the answer, but his words reflected only his roots across the river in Phenix City, Alabama.

He shrugged his shoulders and said, "I guess you have to have somebody to be better than."

We continued our search at the libraries and

Floyd McNeese and son-in-law Mitch Southall on the western bank

museums and archives all along the river. When we had finished, we found the Chattahoochee at the root of the states' rocky relationship. All controversies, stereotypes, and jokes associated with the two states seem to have originated with the river.

The story begins in 1802 when the state of Georgia ceded all of its territory west of the Chattahoochee to the United States. To this day, Alabamians should curse Georgia's three commissioners who drafted the article of cession with federal representatives. Although no permanent white settlements existed along the Chattahoochee at the time, Georgians James Jackson, Abraham Baldwin, and John Milledge knew that whatever authority controlled the river would

Fred Fussell at Eagle-Phenix Dam

also control commerce. River travel was the swiftest means of transport, and hydropower was essential to any industrial endeavor. With this point in mind, the statesmen claimed the Chattahoochee for Georgia and set the boundary as "running thence up the said River Chatta-hoochee and along the western bank thereof." Some fifty years later, this language would prove critical in maintaining Georgia's sovereignty over the entire river and handicapping Alabama economically for years to come.

In 1819, Alabama entered the Union, and white settlers began pouring into the area. In 1828 the city of Columbus was laid out on the east bank of the river at the edge of the new frontier. The same year, the river's first dam was constructed in Columbus to power a grist mill. The paddlewheeler *Fanny* arrived in town as well, becoming the first steamboat to ply the river from the Gulf of Mexico to the fall line. Soon Columbus was a bustling and increasingly prosperous frontier town.

On the opposite shore, the Alabama town of Girard (later Phenix City) sprang up and quickly earned an unsavory reputation among the upstanding Georgians in Columbus. Though Alabama was already incorporated as a state, it was the Wild West in those days—home to the Creek Indians and also to a passel of lawless whites and runaway slaves (and a few hardworking, God-fearing families). When righteous men on the Georgia side wished to settle a dispute with a pistol duel, they crossed the river to a spot in Alabama, where laws prohibiting such activity could not be enforced.

In one memorable episode during 1828, George Walker Crawford, Georgia's attorney general, shot and killed Thomas Edgehill Burnside, also an attorney, over a dispute involving an insult to Crawford's father that had been published in an Augusta newspaper. Crawford, having proved his chivalry, went on to become Georgia's governor and in 1861 the chairman of the Georgia Secession Convention.

Columbus's neighbor city to the west became so disreputable that it was known as Sodom. In 1932, a Swedish scholar named C. D. Arfwedson traveled through the area and described life on the Alabama shore:

> Scarcely a day passed without some human blood being shed in the vicinity; and not satisfied with murdering each other, they cross the river clandestinely and pursue their bloody vocation even in Columbus. With such neighbors, it certainly is not surprising that the city of Columbus should preserve a certain uncouthness of manners, peculiar to a place that has just sprung up in a forest, but which, from its rapid progress, ought to have already disappeared, if the vicinity of Sodom had not to a certain degree retarded the advance of civilization.

While Sodom retarded the cultural growth of Georgia's newest boomtown, Georgia retarded economic growth along the Alabama shore by claiming the entire river. Riverfront lots in Columbus extended across the river to the Alabama shore. Lacking access to the river, residents of Girard were denied the right to build wharfs, bridges, or dams—construction of the sort that was fast turning Columbus into an economic machine.

The controversy came to a head in the 1840s when Columbusite John H. Howard and Girard resident Stephen M. Ingersoll butted heads in a comical tale of dueling lawsuits. In 1845, Howard constructed a four-foot dam across the width of the Chattahoochee. Some 300 yards upriver at the base of the western bank, Ingersoll, without regard for Georgia's claim to the river, prior to 1842 had built a mill that harnessed the river's power. When the water began rising be-

hind Howard's dam, it quickly inundated Ingersoll's mill, rendering it inoperable. Ingersoll promptly filed suit against Howard in Alabama courts and won $4,000 in damages before a jury of his Alabama peers.

Meanwhile, Howard filed suit in Georgia, claiming that Ingersoll had not only trespassed upon his property (the river) but had also caught fish during the commission of this crime. The friendly Georgia jury awarded Howard $600 in damages.

Both cases wound their way through the lower courts and eventually came before the U.S. Supreme Court in 1851. The justices of the court were left with the unenviable task of accurately defining the boundary between the two states. At issue was what had been meant in 1802 by the phrase "running thence up the said Chattahoochee River and along the western bank thereof."

Alabama interpreted the phrase to mean where the water met the shore at ordinary low water. Such an interpretation would allow the state access to the river, since ordinary low water left much of the western bed and bank high and dry for most of the year.

Georgia argued before the Supreme Court that the "boundary line runs along the *top* of the high western bank, leaving the bed of the river and the western shelving shore within the jurisdiction of Georgia."

The high court, with Justice James Moore Wayne giving the opinion, found both interpretations incorrect and ruled, after consulting nearly a dozen definitions of "river," "riverbed," and "riverbank," that the true boundary lay along the base of the western bank.

"It is plain that the western limit of Georgia on and along the bank of the river, must be where the bank and the water meet in its bed within the natural channel or passage of the river," wrote Justice Wayne. "'Along the bank' is strong and definite enough to exclude the idea that any part of the river or its bed was not to be within the state of Georgia."

Georgia thus came to control the river, thanks to a carefully worded article of cession. The unfairness of the boundary was not lost on the justices, however. Noting that other states sharing a river as a boundary used the middle of the river as the state line, Justice Samuel Nelson wrote, "No one can set up a claim to an exclusive right to the flow of all the water in its natural state. . . . Streams of water are intended for the use and comfort of man; and it would be unreasonable, and contrary to the universal sense of mankind, to debar a riparian proprietor from the application of the water to domestic, agricultural, and manufacturing purposes, provided the use works no substantial injury to others."

Alabama challenged the boundary line before the U.S. Supreme Court again in 1859. Ironically, when the two states called upon the federal court to settle their boundary dispute, they were both preparing to secede from the Union. The high court reaffirmed its findings in the initial case but noted that residents of both states retained the right to navigate the river.

From that time forward, economic development on the Alabama shore was in leg irons, and the cultural and educational strides that naturally accompany economic prosperity also lagged. As long as the river remained essential for economic growth, the state of Alabama would trail Georgia. Unfortunately for Alabamians, the river remained the cornerstone of the economy into the twentieth century.

Today's economic statistics bear the imprint of this early controversy between the states. In 1990, Georgia's gross state product of $136 billion was nearly double that of Alabama. The per capita statistics are even more telling. Each Georgian produced $21,129 in 1990, making the state twenty-second among the fifty states. The same year, each Alabamian produced $17,410. The state's rank? Forty-sixth among the fifty states.

Statistics tell a similar story in the arena of education. In Georgia, 71 percent of the population twenty-five years or older held high school diplomas in 1990. In Alabama, it was 67 percent. In Georgia, over 19 percent of the population twenty-five or older held a bachelor's degree or higher. In Alabama, it was less than 16 percent. Georgia pays its public school teachers more and has more institutions of higher education.

In category after category, Alabama bears the scars inflicted by three Georgia statesmen intent on controlling the Chattahoochee in 1802. And to this day, the "Welcome to Georgia" road signs stand on the river's western bank.

The court rulings have made the riverside landscape in Columbus and Phenix City a study in contrasts. Water on the river's east bank laps at the brick foundations of Columbus's mills. The west bank is wooded and as wild as a metropolitan riverbank can be, or at least it was until Phenix City began developing its river walk after our journey. By 1998, much of the west bank's wildness was tamed and landscaped.

"I'm glad it happened that way," Fussell told us of the river of his youth. "Our side of the river was wild, pretty, and accessible, so I romped around along the river as a kid."

By the time the young Fussell was tramping along Phenix City's riverbank in the early 1950s, his town had discovered businesses that the river could not govern—prostitution, gambling, and the dispensing of spirits. Clubs like Ma Beachie's Swing Club, Shad's Rose Room, and the Plantation Club serviced the boys in training across the river at Fort Benning. During World War II and the Korean War, the recruits' numbers swelled into the tens of thousands, and they poured over the bridges from Columbus like one of the river's winter floods. Phenix City was a bustling town, if slightly seedy, and its reputation became such that a military pontoon bridge spanning the river from the fort earned the name "Whiskey Bridge."

Fussell, just a preteen at the time, clearly recalls those days.

"I can remember seeing posters of the strippers along the Fourteenth Street Bridge," he said. "But I didn't know that Phenix City was any different than anyplace else until the town was put under marshal law. I was about twelve when that happened."

The events that led Alabama governor Gordon Persons to declare marshal law in the town may very well haunt Phenix City forever. In the wild frontier town atmosphere, big bucks and gambling bosses made political corruption the norm. The city became an embarrassment to the state. During the 1954 Democratic primary election for state attorney general, Phenix City lawyer Albert Patterson successfully campaigned on a promise to clean up his own town. Days after winning the primary, he was shot and killed on the street in front of his Phenix City office.

Governor Persons responded by calling in the troops, which collected dozens of slot machines and other gaming paraphernalia and set them ablaze behind the county courthouse. Pouring licenses were revoked, the city commission was removed from office, and the Fort Benning soldiers were turned back at the bridges spanning the river. Albert Fuller, Russell County's deputy sheriff, was later arrested and convicted of the murder. A book was published on this dark chapter in history and also a movie, more fiction than fact, entitled *The Phenix City Story.* The grade B film painted the town as "Sin City" and spread its infamy across the country. These events further boosted Georgia's sense of cultural and even moral superiority.

Lee Lott, a Phenix City businessman who served as mayor in the late 1960s, was a young man at the time. He grew up downtown, and today when he introduces himself to strangers his roots almost always elicit lively conversation. People still think of the town as Sin City even though no bar served a single mixed drink there from 1954 to 1968. But for Lott, as for everyone else who lived in the town during the era, the events of the 1950s remain etched in memory. In fact, the day after Patterson's murder, Lott dined with Deputy Sheriff Fuller at the town's legendary Elite Café—next door to Patterson's law office and the scene of the crime.

"Phenix City has always been unfairly labeled," Lott said, "mainly because of that 1954 problem. We've never been able to live it down. We've always been sort of the stepchild of Alabama. The old saying goes that Alabama didn't want us and Georgia couldn't have us."

Still, Lott remembers fondly the days when the rowdy soldiers roamed his town. He and friends would set up shop on the streets leading from Columbus and shine the boots of Patton's army during the war.

"We could earn twenty-five dollars in two days, charging twenty-five cents for shoes and thirty cents for boots," he said. When the boys shined paratrooper's boots, they used latex condoms to blouse the pants of the paratroopers

Lee Lott at Phenix City's Elite Café

over their calf-length boots. Of course, with 50,000 young soldiers in the area, condoms were as readily available as rubber bands, and they worked better.

During the war it was something else to behold. They'd come to Phenix City and raise hell, and they didn't care whether they got locked up or not. They knew they faced death on the battlefield. They'd get off the bus in Columbus, and by the time they got to Phenix City, they'd already passed fifty liquor stores. It was just a bad time and place for an eighteen-year-old headed for Europe or the Pacific. It was their first time away from home, first time getting drunk, their first time with a girl.

I grew up on Broad Street, and the G.I.s would pass out and crawl up under the front porch. I'd wake up in the morning and there'd be one or two under the porch sometimes, especially on pay days. Mom would call taxi cabs for them to take them back so they wouldn't wind up AWOL.

The year after the state ran the gambling, prostitution, and corruption out of town, *Look* magazine awarded Phenix City its All-American City Award for the townspeople's efforts to restore civil living, but even such national publicity couldn't undo the damage that had already been done. Today many people still act as if the infamous events of 1954 had occurred only recently.

Fussell, undaunted by his connection with the tainted town, enrolled at the University of Alabama, where he studied art and learned that his hometown's reputation reached far and wide. "There were always jokes, especially if I wanted to get in a card game," he said. "It was always in jest but not completely. Everybody that grew up there experienced those type things. People wondered whether you were a person that could be trusted—whether you could turn your back on this person. It kind of gave you an edge—watch your step around me because I know some things that you don't know."

When Fussell returned to his hometown, he worked as an artist, illustrating training manuals for the army. Today he likes to claim that "everyone that went to Vietnam had my drawings in their back pockets."

Some forty years after Patterson's murder, the strip clubs and bars serving the boys at Fort Benning now line Victory Drive in Columbus, the main thoroughfare to the military base. Liquor and other delights are served up in Georgia, and Phenix City is quiet, with hardly a soldier in sight.

Today the economic tables are beginning to turn. The river, though important to economic development, is no longer as essential as it was in the 1800s. Businesses looking for new locations are swayed as much by lucrative tax laws and other state subsidies. Recently Alabama has been aggressive in courting new industries.

Alabama used state-backed incentives to land Mercedes Benz's first American assembly plant, and Phenix City, in spite of its inferiority complex, enticed Mead, the paper products giant, to relocate its regional headquarters in town along the river's bank. Even Phenix City's wild and wooded riverfront has undergone a transfor-

mation. Keeping pace with Columbus's riverfront development, the city has created its own river walk plus an amphitheater. Long handicapped, Alabama is catching up. During recent years, the state's growth in per capita income has outpaced Georgia's. Through the early 1990s, Alabama saw the number of its citizens living in poverty fall while Georgia's poverty rate climbed.

Downriver from Columbus and Phenix City, Walter F. George Lock and Dam and the lake they form stands as yet another testament to the states' adversarial relationship. During the mid-1960s, as the lake was being impounded, politicians on both sides of the river became engaged in a lake-naming battle.

Shortly after the dam's completion, Georgia's Department of Transportation began erecting road signs near the reservoir that designated it "Lake Chattahoochee." On the Alabama side, the state General Assembly passed a bill designating the name Lake Eufaula, honoring the Alabama town overlooking the lake. Congress alone had the power to name the lake, however.

Residents lobbied for names like Lake Chattahoochee, Lake Alaga (a politically correct combination of the state names), and Lake Henry-Clay—a name that combined the two states' counties most inundated by the dam's floodwater.

A worker at the dam's powerhouse during the controversy, sarcastically proposed the name "Lake Screamer" to honor the tiny lakeside Alabama community where he lived. He emblazoned the bumper of his truck with a tag that read "Lake Screamer."

Eventually the states agreed to disagree. Congress officially named the lock and dam for Georgia senator Walter F. George. The states now use different names for the reservoir. Today, if you're on the Alabama side, you can buy a map of the lake that's labeled "Lake Eufaula." Travel a mile across river to Georgetown and the same map, from the same publisher, is labeled "Lake Walter F. George."

The latest controversy between the states of course revolves once again around the Chattahoochee. When metropolitan Atlanta petitioned the Corps of Engineers to increase its water withdrawals from the river, Alabama filed a lawsuit to keep it from doing so. A long court battle was averted in the early 1990s when the two states and Florida agreed to the Comprehensive Tri-State Water Study of the Chattahoochee River basin but not before the states' bureaucrats had fired a few salvos at each other.

Upon learning of Alabama's lawsuit, Georgia Department of Natural Resources Commissioner Leonard Ledbetter, citing Georgia's century-old claim of ownership to all the river's water, dispatched letters to Alabama's Mead Paper Company and Alabama Power's Farley Nuclear Power Plant. He demanded that the businesses obtain water withdrawal and discharge permits from Georgia and threatened them with daily fines of up to $50,000 for failure to act. Ledbetter later admitted that his demands were a tit-for-tat response to the lawsuit.

By the time we reached the Florida/Alabama state line twenty-five miles above Jim Woodruff Dam, we'd heard dozens of Alabama jokes and had concluded that people are pretty much the same on either side of the river. According to current lifestyle statistics, residents of the two states are quite similar. Per capita beer consumption, percentage of smokers, and divorce rate, for example, are virtually the same in both states. Even the percentage of households without indoor plumbing or telephones is comparable.

Fussell, the Phenix City native and folklorist who studies the culture of the Chattahoochee Valley, concurs. "The river really doesn't make that much difference," he told us. "Historically, the river has been something that bound the people together rather than separated the people."

In fact, the statistics show that some of the Alabama jokes we heard might be more appropriate with Georgia as the butt rather than Alabama. One joke runs: "What do you call a fortune cookie in Alabama?" The answer? "A biscuit with a food stamp in it." The truth? U.S. Bureau of Census statistics show that for 1992, 8.5 percent of Georgia's population received public aid as compared with 7.1 percent of Alabama's population.

Another joke goes: "Did you hear about the tornado that ripped through Alabama?" The answer is: "Yep, they're still searching for the governor's mansion. The twister ripped it right off its wheels and blocks." The truth? Figures show that per capita mobile home ownership in the two states is virtually identical.

Still, Georgians can choose to ignore the facts. After all, we have to feel better than someone.

Maple at Mossy Creek, Hall County

Dogwood and spanish moss at Riverbend, Russell County

Spring at Devil's Racecourse Shoals, Fulton County

Maples at Medlock Bridge, Gwinnett County

Rock and fall reflections at Medlock Bridge, Gwinnett County

CLOCKWISE FROM TOP LEFT: *Reflections in the Chattahoochee National Forest, White County;*
Shoals at the mouth of Peachtree Creek, Fulton County; Morning reflections at Jones Bridge, Fulton County;
Spring reflections at Island Ford, Fulton County

Morning on Goat Rock Lake, Lee County

Falling Branches, Fulton County

Sunset at Jones Bridge, Gwinnett County

Sunset at Rogers Bridge, Fulton County

Morning at Bull Sluice Lake, Fulton County

CHAPTER NINE

CRITTERS

IN THE COASTAL PLAIN, THE RIVER GROWS WIDE, DEEP, AND LAZY. IN the vein of stereotypical southern rivers, moss-draped trees grow on its shores, and white sand beaches grow wide in bends where the current cooperates. The mostly wild landscape is interrupted only by the Corps of Engineers' navigation buoys, which designate the river's deepest channel for the river barges that tug up infrequently from Apalachicola.

On the banks, the reflective navigational mile markers that the Corps posted regularly on trees show the mileage from the Gulf. We used these markers to gauge our progress as if we were traveling on a lonesome interstate. Within a mile of leaving the historic steamboat landing in Columbus, we realized that the river would no longer be the fast-moving, shoal-filled stream to which we had grown accustomed during the previous two months of paddling through the mountains and piedmont.

Another keen difference below the fall line was that we no longer sat at the top of the food chain. When we paddled away from Columbus, past the town's river walk and into the first secluded stretches of the Lower Chattahoochee on the coastal plain, we entered alligator country.

We have never been disturbed by the idea of sharing the woods with bears during our hikes on the Appalachian Trail. Bears, and eastern black bears in particular, are mostly herbivorous. They don't usually bother humans. Alligators, on the other hand, are card-carrying carnivores. Their prehistoric career was so successful that they survived to the present largely unchanged. Given the opportunity, they can and will indulge in human flesh; they have eighty teeth, for heaven's sake. Granted, alligator attacks on humans are rare. Through the early 1990s, only a few incidents were reported to authorities in Georgia—none of which occurred on the Chattahoochee and none of which resulted in fatalities. Nevertheless, we were humbled and intimidated by the prospect of venturing into territory where we might encounter a predator. The gator country of the Southeast's rivers, swamps, and marshlands is the only place in the eastern United States where humans can not only taste the wild but also be tasted by it.

Being born in the piedmont and finding our first outdoor adventures in the mountains, we had an inherent lack of familiarity with alligators that left us with a slightly irrational fear of the creatures.

In the days leading up to our departure from Columbus, we were warned repeatedly: "Watch out for the alligators south of here." The fourteen-foot gator stuffed and on display at the Columbus Museum did little to allay our fears; it was only three feet shorter than our boat. We floated south of Columbus, alert to the slightest movement at the water's edge and prepared for a surprise attack.

At the mouth of Upatoi Creek ten miles downstream from the fall line city, the river enters the U.S. Army's Fort Benning complex, a sprawling 184,000-acre training ground for our troops. We heard the soldiers before we saw

them. One was carrying on a tirade with more foul language than an Eddie Murphy monologue. We thought a drill sergeant was barking orders, but when we rounded the bend, we found an off-duty soldier in fatigues fishing with his comrades. We drifted by quietly, and he didn't miss an expletive.

Later, we were buzzed by choppers and planes in training. We watched as the big planes ejected hundreds of paratroopers, one after another, their chutes opening in regimented order, in stark contrast to the chaotic, wild woods that seemed to swallow them.

Fort Benning, named in honor of the distinguished Confederate commander Henry L. Benning, has been a part of the river's landscape since 1918. Through the late 1950s, a pontoon bridge spanned the river and was used by the army in training exercises. In 1939, when Caraker Paschal and Minton Braddy floated the river from Atlanta to the Gulf, this bridge created one of their trip's most memorable moments.

"A major was making moving pictures of the soldiers crossing it," Paschal wrote in an account published in the *Atlanta Journal* in 1939.

He ordered us to get out of the river so we wouldn't interfere. We sat on the bank until the game grew monotonous. Then a couple of soldiers told us they would help us across the bridge. We had the rowboat in the middle of the bridge when a platoon of soldiers started across from the opposite side.

The leading soldiers had to stop when they reached the boat, and since they were bunched up, the pontoons under them began to sink. Another group stopped about 10 yards behind them, and so on across the river, each crowd forcing a section of the bridge underwater. . . . One fellow got scared and dropped his helmet into the river.

All the soldiers on shore were having a big laugh, except the major. Only those who have heard a major relieve his feelings can imagine the things he said.

I suppose soldiers always have cursed like sailors and always will.

That night we camped on a marshy island at the mouth of Uchee Creek where the army operates a soldiers-only recreation area. We had considered camping in the recreation area until we learned that it was off limits to civilians. Instead the workers there directed us to the island at the creek's mouth. It looked friendly and flat enough.

We paddled through high marshy grass to reach its shore, and when we made landfall, we heard a loud crash and splash nearby, as if we'd disturbed something very large.

"What was that?" Monica asked, alarmed.

"Alligator?" I suggested.

"Could be a deer," Monica countered hopefully.

Despite our gatorphobia, we went ashore, set up our domed tent, cooked our dinner, and listened to the disturbing, staccato beat of artillery fire and automatic weapons used in training as they competed with a deafening chorus of frogs.

Snug inside our tent at nightfall, we began hearing the same loud rustling that we'd heard upon our landing. We knew the sounds of opossums, raccoons, and skunks in the night, but this was different. It was a clumsy noise—distant at first, but creeping ever closer to our synthetic home. Our minds began to race, and our heartbeats quickened. "Can gators bite through nylon and no-see-um netting?" "Maybe it would prefer some trail mix to a human leg?"

"Could be a deer," I suggested, mimicking Monica's earlier wish.

We realized it would be a sleepless night until we knew for sure. We mustered the courage to unzip our tent and cautiously stepped outside armed only with our flashlight. Our beam quickly found its target. We faced not the eerie glow of gator eyes. Instead a harmless armadillo stared back at us, seeming annoyed by our intrusion.

Armadillos, long associated with the Southwest, have migrated east during the past seventy years. Populations in south Georgia and Alabama have skyrocketed in the past ten years. In the

Armadillo

area's soft, sandy soil, the animals have found pleasant digging. Their sensitive noses and long tongues allow them to scarf up beetles, centipedes, grasshoppers, and any other insect they stumble across. They've become so common in the area that they've displaced opossums as the number one roadkill. When frightened, they often jump straight up into the air. On the road, this habit translates into jumping directly into oncoming headlights.

Though the armor-coated rodent doesn't look like much of a swimmer, the armadillo can inflate its gut, adding buoyancy to a body that would otherwise sink like an anchor. This trait has of course helped the animal migrate east of the Mississippi and enabled our friend to startle us at our island campsite.

Armadillos ultimately caused us more headaches than gators. They fearlessly scrambled through our campsites, oblivious to our presence, and roused us from our sleep. We still can't figure out how an animal that usually weighs about twelve pounds can make so much noise. On more than one occasion, we'd wake to discover that the creatures had dug up the catholes that we used as wilderness water closets.

Still, we never completely overcame our gator fears. "Swim at your own risk" and "Don't feed the alligators" signs at state parks didn't help. We did, however, see dozens of the creatures. In one day alone on Lake Seminole, we counted more than two dozen. If we spotted them on shore, they would dash into the water and swim out of sight. If we saw their snouts forming V-shaped wakes, they would dive and hide. We quickly learned that they were as afraid of us as we were of them.

On Lake Eufaula, we camped on the sandbar of a small island where a large dead catfish lay bleached, bloated, and rotting. Out of noseshot of the stench, we enjoyed a broccoli and pasta dinner on an unusually cool June evening. The next morning, when we went to inspect the catfish, we found in its place the unmistakable claw and tail prints of an alligator. We determined that the moral of the story was to never lay around on a beach in gator country looking like a bloated, dead catfish.

Not until we had reached the lower stretches of the Apalachicola did we enjoy a close encounter with one of the reptiles. We were paddling on the river's eastern shore in the early morning to avoid the sun, searching for the yellow crowned night herons and egrets that patrolled the shallows for shellfish. Without warning, a seven-foot alligator surfaced within inches of our canoe, so close that we withdrew our paddles for fear of bumping it. It swam along beside us for several seconds, seeming unaware of our presence. Monica could have reached out and pulled its tail. I could have scratched its head. When the creature finally spotted us, it flipped its tail and sped underwater. We took a deep breath.

Thirty years ago, gators were rarely seen on the river. Rozelle and Kuniansky didn't recall seeing any during their 1972 expedition. Originally granted federal protection in 1967, the reptiles have made a tremendous comeback on the Chattahoochee. The numbers on Lake Seminole are such that the state of Florida sponsors an annual hunt.

Beavers, muskrats, mink, raccoons, deer, coyotes, river cooters, alligator snapping turtles, tree frogs, brown water snakes, kingfishers, crawfish—the list of creatures that we encountered seemed endless. And which of the river's creatures was most ubiquitous? Oddly, it was the

Alligator

domesticated cow. Cows occupy every flood-plain pasture from White County, Georgia, to Gulf County, Florida.

The diversity of wildlife was so great that every bend of the river seemed to hold another discovery. The sheer number of the creatures we saw made the 3 million or so humans that drink the river's water seem insignificant. Billions of creatures not only lap up the cool waters but also call them home.

When we pushed off from the river's source at 3,500 feet above sea, we fished salamanders out of Chattahoochee Spring. These were the river's first residents. As we reached the mouth of the river at Apalachicola and paddled beneath the U.S. Route 98 bridge into the bay, a pair of bottle-nosed dolphins surfaced in front of our canoe as if to greet us at our journey's end.

Modern science, with its microbiologists and genetic physicists, has demystified much of nature. We've gone above and beyond Darwin in our understanding of the natural world, and we've explained the seemingly inexplicable ways of wilderness. Native Americans, including the Creeks of the Chattahoochee Valley, used myths and spirits to account for mysterious natural phenomena. Today we need only flip through our Audubon field guides. We used several on this journey religiously. Though we usually found the answers to our questions, we couldn't help but classify some of what we witnessed as miracles plain and simple. "Nature," Thomas Wolfe once wrote, "is the one place where miracles not only happen, they happen all the time."

Take, for example, the American eel. We'd never seen the creature until we beached our canoe next to a family of cane-pole fishermen on the banks of the Apalachicola near Blue Spring sandbar.

When we hopped out to say hello, we stumbled upon a snakelike fish lying on the bank near a large woman perched squarely atop a five-gallon bucket. The eel, with its dorsal fin running the length of its back, gasped for breath using its overshot lower jaw.

"What in the hell is that?" I asked, somewhat shocked and frightened.

"Oooooo, it's an eel," she said. "It's poisonous! I just cut it right off the line; didn't even touch it. I ain't messin' with it. Some people eat 'em, but it looks too much like a snake for me."

We picked it up and brushed off the dirt sticking to its smooth, slimy skin.

The American eel lives one of the most unusual lives of any of the river's marine animals. It is a catadromous species, which means that the adults inhabit the rivers of the Atlantic and Gulf coasts but swim to sea to spawn, reversing the usual route taken by fish. The females, followed by the males, leave the Apalachicola and swim more than 1,000 miles to a spot in the Atlantic Ocean called the Sargasso Sea. There the exhausted adults spawn and die. The tiny fry, on their own and awash in a vast ocean, somehow manage to return to their home rivers in a migration that can take up to two years. They live out their adult lives in the rivers until the primal urge drives them back to the Sargasso.

We left the eel with the fisherwoman. For her, it was as mysterious as it must have been to the Creek and Seminole Indians. It probably became gator food that night on the bank of the river. The American eel, far from being poisonous, is quite tasty. Eels are considered a delicacy in European countries, but squeamishness has kept them from becoming familiar to most American palates.

The gar, more common on the Chattahoochee than the eel, is equally reviled. We saw the prehistoric creatures everywhere. A two-foot specimen chased my fishing lure to within four feet of the shore as I cast from a sandbar south of

Columbus. On several other occasions, gar more than four feet long surfaced near our vessel, creating tremendous, frightening wakes.

Lamar Cobb, a hog, cattle, cotton, and peanut farmer who works land along the river in Seminole County, claimed he once netted a seven-foot gar. "I thought it was going to make me get out of the boat," he said. "But I flipped it

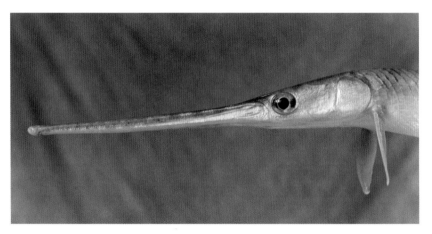

Long-nosed Gar

over into the boat and it just laid there. Didn't flop at all." He loaded it into the back of his pickup and hauled it around Donalsonville, showing off the unusual creature.

On the Chattahoochee and Apalachicola, gar come in several varieties, all characterized by long, slender bodies, armorlike scales, and elongated snouts filled with dozens of razor-sharp teeth. The alligator gar, the largest of the species, can reach lengths of ten feet and can weigh more than 200 pounds. Apart from the bowfin, no other fish found in the Chattahoochee has been changed less by evolution. Gar are aquatic dinosaurs that refused to die. Catfish are endearingly ugly. Gar are just plain ugly. No other fish elicited more spirited comments from the anglers we met.

"I'm afraid of them, to tell you the truth."

"Scary fish."

"You'll be in the fight for your life if you ever hook one."

"I caught one yesterday. Somebody told me it was a delicacy so I fried it up, but an old fried innertube would have tasted better."

"The meat's as white as cotton and delicious if you know how to fix it."

The lowly catfish, served on all-you-can-eat fried platters across the South, is the signature fish of the river, but from our view, the much-maligned gar seems more appropriate. It was eaten by the Creeks, who used the sharp teeth in numerous rituals. Unruly children were disciplined by raking their legs with the teeth. The stamina and strength of warriors and ball players could be improved by a similar method, the Creeks believed, and those same teeth were used in an excruciating form of capital punishment; a single tooth was used to make a deep cut from the back of the head, down the back and leg, severing the Achilles tendon. The disabled criminal was then turned loose to die.

Despite the gar's reputation as a fierce fighter, today's sportsmen rarely pursue it. Its teeth make it difficult to catch by conventional methods, and its tough skin and scales make dressing it a test of strength and patience. Tin snips and an ax are the recommended tools, but when it is prepared properly, the white meat is said to have the consistency and flavor of shrimp. You may classify the gar among the Rodney Dangerfields of the fish world, but unless you believe the myths of giant man-eating catfish, this is the big daddy of the river's fish.

Overhead, birds of all kinds entertained us. Near Fort Gaines, and directly below the Georgia Route 37 bridge over the river leading into the town, we watched a comical encounter between a broad-winged hawk and a great blue heron. The hawk dive-bombed the heron incessantly and fi-

nally took up a perch on driftwood at the river's edge a few feet from the larger bird. The heron croaked in protest each time the hawk made a foray. They argued back and forth for several minutes before the heron flew off, defeated. The nature of the dispute remained a mystery to us.

By the end of our trip we had positively identified more than seventy different species of birds, and if we had been true birders, we could easily have doubled the figure. In Florida's Apalachicola River basin alone, more than 300 different species have been sighted.

Without a doubt, the most beautiful bird we saw was the swallow-tail kite of the Apalachicola River's swampland. Our Golden Field Guide described it as "the most graceful of North American hawks," but this phrase doesn't do the bird justice. While we prisoners of gravity reclined on the Apalachicola's sandbars, the kites slipped in and out of the trees overhead, entertaining us with their acrobatics. With their four-foot wingspans and slender, split tails, they skillfully worked the air, changing direction in a flash to snag a cicada or a toad from a treetop. Eagles and hawks look slow and awkward alongside kites. Kites are so at home in the air that they can eat most of their prey while still in flight, unlike their more powerful but less agile winged relatives.

The osprey, the dean of the river's birds of prey, doesn't require as much finesse. It earns its keep with a keen eye, persistence, and power. On more than one occasion, we watched as the fish hawk hovered above the river and then half-folded its wings to begin a rapid, ear-popping descent to the water's surface. The birds would hit the water with a splash, often completely submerging themselves, and then flap away with a fish secured in their talons.

Ospreys take any fish they can find—bowfin,

carp, catfish, or eel—and can lift prey of up to six pounds, more than twice the bird's own body weight. Ornithologists have described the bird as "peaceful, gentle and harmless" for its Mister Rogers–like ways. These large birds often share their treetop nests with sparrows, wrens, and small herons, which use the nest's lower levels.

If left alone, the osprey sticks to hunting—a task that it pursues with unparalleled industry. More often than not, however, the osprey is pestered by the bald eagle, itself a less than industrious hunter.

The most endearing characteristic of the bald eagle, our popularly revered national symbol since 1782, is its good looks. Underneath the grand black and white exterior lurks a shiftless, lazy fowl. Eagles are the osprey's worst enemy. In an avian form of robbery, they stake out osprey nests and dive-bomb the smaller birds, forcing their victims to drop any fish that they may be carrying. Ospreys can rarely escape this larceny.

On Lake Eufaula, we ran into Sara Glass, a park ranger and biologist with the Corps of Engineers, who just grinned when we mentioned the thievery of the eagle.

Glass, who was tracking five nesting sites around the lake, said, "It's amazing to me that they made it as the national bird. They harass other birds for food. They're scavengers. They're very lazy birds. They even run vultures off their kills."

Arthur Clevland Bent, who wrote the book *Life Histories of North American Birds of Prey,* was equally critical of the bald eagle. "Its carrion-feeding habits, its timid and cowardly behavior and its predatory attacks on the smaller and weaker osprey hardly inspire respect and certainly do not exemplify the best in American character. . . . Eagles have always been looked upon as emblems of power and valor, so our na-

tional bird may still be admired by those who are not familiar with its habits."

Sure enough, the only time we saw a bald eagle hunting or feasting, the bird was dining turkey vulture–style atop a rotting fish on a shore of Lake Eufaula. When the bald eagle spotted us, it escaped to a high perch, leaving its lakeside dinner, perhaps scared, perhaps embarrassed.

Ben Franklin, who regarded the bald eagle as a "bird of bad moral character," suggested making the wild turkey our national symbol, a choice we endorse on the basis of our experiences on the river. If you disregard the face and neck, turkeys equal the bald eagles in beauty of plumage. In fact, the turkey's head alone should have gotten it nominated for at least the back of a dollar bill; it's colored red, white, and blue. Furthermore, in all likelihood, both the Declaration of Independence and the Constitution were penned and signed using turkey quills. And contrary to popular belief, turkeys are quite majestic in flight.

On the backwaters of Lake Harding near the mill village of Riverview, Alabama, we watched drop-jawed as one of the twenty-pound turkeys soared across the river, looking very much like a bird of prey. Though the turkey prefers to run (and does so quite well, reaching speeds up to fifteen miles an hour), bursts from its powerful wings can carry it on nonstop flights of a mile or more.

On another occasion we spotted a wild turkey in the Palisades unit of the national recreation area in Atlanta. That we saw one of the birds in the midst of a large metropolitan area, and within a half mile of rush hour traffic on the state's busiest highways, is a testament to the birds' adaptability and persistence. It's hard to believe that the birds were almost driven to extinction in the South within the last century.

Nevertheless, some bird watchers would scoff at the thought of placing the turkey on coins and bills and seals. Bent, while denouncing the bald eagle, wrote of the turkey, "such a vain and pompous fowl would have been a worse choice." Many seasoned turkey hunters will tell you that the only thing that can possibly be mistaken for a courting turkey is a stumping politician.

Another animal that perhaps should have gotten a few nods as a national emblem is the beaver. In Canada, the rodent did achieve such status. Perhaps no other animal played a greater role in the exploration and colonization of the United States and Canada, for the beaver pelt trade of the eighteenth and nineteenth centuries brought trappers farther and farther into the continent's interior.

On the Chattahoochee, as on all large rivers where deep water is plentiful, the beavers inhabit burrows dug into the riverbank rather than lodges of mud and sticks. We saw them regularly, particularly in the seventy miles of flowing river south of Atlanta where the abundant cottonwoods, birch, and poplar keep the bank beavers fat and happy. On one occasion, we paddled within feet of one that appeared to be taking a midday siesta on the riverbank in Fulton County. Waking suddenly as we approached, it quickly sought safety underwater.

At night, the distinctive warning whack of the beaver's tail on the water often startled us, and by day we saw constant reminders of their industry in the smooth, bleached wood of meticulously chewed tree trunks. More than once, we took advantage of their well-worn trails through the thick riverbank undergrowth.

Today, when we talk with schoolchildren about the river, we ask them what animal is most like them. They typically answer, as do most adults, by naming a primate. The correct answer, of course, is the beaver. Excepting hu-

Beaver

mans, no other mammal does more to shape its environment, and thus the beaver has appropriately been called nature's original engineer. Beavers clear-cut forests like paper companies, construct recreational impoundments like the Corps of Engineers, and build homes like suburban land developers. Ironically, the beaver has a terribly small brain.

But unlike the endeavors of big-brained humans, the beaver's work has historically benefited the landscape. The small-scale dams on river tributaries create wetlands that trap silt, prevent streambed erosion, and provide habitat for dozens of other animals. The beaver is one of nature's check valves for clean water: it is a keystone species. The same can hardly be said of humans.

Water oak at Abbotts Bridge, Gwinnett County

Spanish moss near Cliatt Branch, Russell County

Moon at sunrise near Abbotts Bridge, Gwinnett County

Morning near mouth of Cauley Creek, Gwinnett County

Sandbar on the Apalachicola River

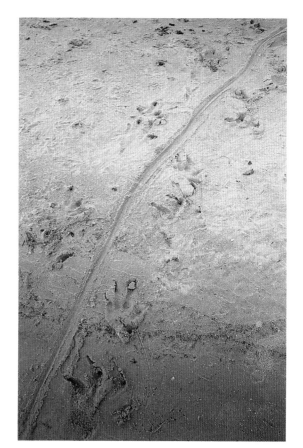  

LEFT TO RIGHT: *Alligator tracks on Lake Eufaula; Raccoon tracks on a sandbar, Henry County; Snake track on a sandbar, Gadsden County*

Upper falls on Mulberry Creek, Harris County

Azalea and rock face at Mulberry Falls, Harris County

Morning at Horseshoe Rapid, White County

Morning near John Creek, Hall County

CHAPTER TEN

FISHERMEN

THE FIRST PEOPLE WE ENCOUNTERED ON OUR JOURNEY ONCE WE LEFT the well-traveled Appalachian Trail at the top of the watershed were trout fishermen— a father and his two sons from nearby Towns County. On a spring morning when the temperature hovered just above freezing, the teenage boys splashed through the river in sneakers and wet jeans. Within minutes, they were reeling in brook trout with their spinning rods.

Around the next bend, at the base of a big falls, we met a walking, talking Orvis advertisement. Outfitted in the best gear the trendy fly-fishing company had to offer, the fisherman gingerly stepped upriver in rubber waders, well protected from the bone-numbing water.

A quarter mile downstream, we met a trio of young men who had come up from Marietta for a weekend camping and fishing expedition. Dressed in flannel, jeans, and camouflage, they worked their corn-baited hooks below a man-made trout bar near the U.S. Forest Service's Upper Chattahoochee River Campground. A Confederate flag waved from a pole in the bed of their Ford pickup, and a sticker on the back bumper said, "You Keep Your X, I'll Keep Mine"—a veiled reference to Malcolm X and the Confederate battle flag steeped in southern pride and bigotry.

The opening week of trout season taught us that fishing, even the white-collar dominated world of trout fishing, knows no socioeconomic or cultural boundaries. The river does not discriminate. It takes all comers and more often than not fills their stringers, creels, live wells, and five-gallon buckets with its bounty.

Like the kingfisher, whose angry chirping and enviable aerial acrobatics accompanied us virtually the length of the river, fishermen were our constant companions. Brothers Todd and A. J. Trees, wearing coonskin caps, fished in the headwaters with their dad, Trent Trees from Kennesaw. Louis Robinson, a seventy-four-year-old Atlantan, threw out his bobber at the mouth of Utoy Creek, escaping his city for the calm of the river. Lorell Cherry of Headland, Alabama, shaded by a straw hat and anchored along the shores of the Lower Chattahoochee in his johnboat, pulled in one catfish after another from the folding lawn chair that he used as a captain's seat. Bruce Covington, well adapted to a birth defect that left him with only one complete arm, showed us a live well full of big river bass on Lake Seminole and joked, "If a one-armed fisherman can catch fish like these, you can too." He hauled us, a pair of bumbling neophytes, along for a late afternoon fishing trip, but even with his skillful guidance, we didn't catch a fish. On the Apalachicola, senior citizen sisters Thelma Barfield and Fausteen Varnum cast their lines for channel cats from an old wooden flat-bottomed boat.

The pursuit of bass, cats, panfish, trout, and other gilled creatures ranks as the nation's sixth most popular recreational activity behind walking, swimming, bicycling, camping, and bowling, according to census figures. More than 40 million Americans call themselves fishermen. Fishing requires no more than a stick, line, hook, and worm grubbed from the creek side, as children

know, or it can involve $20,000 bass boats. Its appeal, as basic as our roots, harks back to our primitive existence as wandering hunter-gatherers. Fishing fulfills our innate need to provide and creates the most intimate of relationships with rivers.

Fishing is so popular, particularly in the water-blessed South, that it has an almost cult-like following. Hats read: "A bad day on the river is better than a good day at work" and "It's not how you fish; it's how you wiggle your worm." T-shirts tell us, "Old fishermen never die, they just smell that way." Bumper stickers proclaim, "Work is for people who don't know how to fish." Foam beer cozies read: "Wanted: Good woman. Must be able to clean, cook, sew, dig worms and clean fish. Must have boat and motor. Please send picture of boat and motor."

Our fishing during this trip was a miserable failure. We caught only one small hybrid bass on Lake Oliver while trolling a plastic grub behind the canoe. Luckily, we didn't plan to live off the river's bounty. Fishing, though partly luck, takes patience and observation; it helps to be able to think like a fish. We thought like photographers.

Others along the Chattahoochee who are able to think like fish have successfully parlayed a passion for fishing into careers—in a couple of cases very lucrative careers. On West Point Lake, we paddled by fishing guide Tommy Mike, who had two boats filled with clients parked over a school of shad, casting for bass. Mike, like the Chattahoochee's other impoundment fishing guides, is partly a product of the Corps of Engineers and the Tennessee Valley Authority. Without the dam builders, the South, virtually devoid of the natural lakes that dot the glacially molded landscape of the northern states, would be a land of streams, rivers, and small farm ponds. Bass fishing guides like Mike would be few and far between if they existed at all.

Between 1950 and 1975, fifty-two major impoundments with reservoir capacities greater than 1 million acre feet were constructed in the United States. The vast bodies of water created

Tommy Mike on West Point Lake

inland fisheries with seemingly unlimited potential and introduced a new era of outdoor recreation. Swift-moving rivers, previously inaccessible except to hardy outdoorsmen, became placid, inviting lakes with boat ramps, docks, and marinas. The oceanlike lakes made the small horsepower johnboat almost obsolete and created a market for fishing vessels with engines of 100 horsepower or more. A steady rise in leisure time in post–World War II America ensured that fishing and man-made lakes would grow together in popularity.

In 1967, a fisherman named Ray Scott had what he called a "mystic kind of vision" in a Mississippi motel room. His idea was to hold a competitive bass fishing tournament in which cheating would be impossible. Soon thereafter he organized the first professional bass fishing tour-

nament and went on to build a bass fishing empire called B.A.S.S., the Bass Anglers Sportsman's Society, an organization that today claims more than 600,000 members and sponsors perhaps the most prestigious event in the world of fishing, the BASS Masters Classic. The winner of this three-day fishing tourney receives more than $100,000.

The sport has a following that is of course local as well as national. On West Point Lake, Mike feeds off the sport's popularity. A LaGrange native, he grew up driving the roads that the lake covered when the Corps closed the floodgates in 1974. While working on his graduate degree in fisheries biology at Auburn University in the early 1970s, he participated in preimpoundment studies. He's used this early knowledge to build a successful business that is now more than twenty years old.

Today he lives on the lake's shore in a 6,000-square-foot home with his wife, Katherine, and three children. His commute to the office is a 100-yard walk to his dock. Indoors, Katherine handles the business end of the operation and prepares lunches for clients. The couple's lakefront spread often surprises the wealthy clients Mike carries fishing.

"I'd like to think it's the house that largemouth and white and hybrid bass built," he told us. "When a neurosurgeon from Atlanta comes for a trip and looks at the house and says, 'I'm in the wrong business,' I kind of shudder.

"It's been a dream come true. I never dreamed I'd be a fishing guide. It just happened. It's an example of being in the right place at the right time."

Mike has carried such notables as Bo Jackson and Joe DiMaggio on trips, and each year he spends about 300 days on the lake. He's caught as many as 223 bass in one day and estimates that he's landed more than 250,000 since he began the business in 1975 when he was working part time as a tennis instructor and part time as a package store clerk.

Though Mike will tell you he's doing what he knows best, he remains a bit incredulous about his occupation. It is easy to understand. After all, he traveled to Auburn on a tennis scholarship. The world of love and deuce is a far cry from plastic worms, spinner baits, and shad.

Below West Point, in the blue-collar textile mill villages of Valley, Alabama, the "King-fisher" of the Chattahoochee's bass fisherman got his start. Since 1955, when Tom Mann emigrated to the mill town from his family farm in Penton, Alabama, his has become a household name, particularly in the homes of bass families.

Mann has won several major bass tournaments, has hosted his own fishing show on ESPN, and has sold millions of fishing lures. His many ventures in the artificial bait business have made him a very wealthy man, but meeting him, you'd hardly know it. Though he's been through the wringer of big business, he doesn't seem to have drifted far from his roots on the farm and in the textile mills. The right-of-ways on U.S. Route 431 in Eufaula, which runs by his home and his tourist stop, Tom Mann's Fish World and Aquarium, are still littered with tufts of cotton from the southeast Alabama farms around him.

Like thousands of other farm families across the Cotton Belt in the mid-twentieth century, Mann left farming for what he hoped would be a better life in the cotton mills.

"The farms just went away, and there was nowhere to go except the mills," he told us. "I couldn't see any future in farming. I saw how hard my daddy had to work just to survive, and there was just no doubt, the mills were the place

to go. That's where everybody went. There's nothing harder than plowing with a mule and chopping cotton, so the mill was pleasure to me."

For a boy who grew up making his own hooks and lines from straight pins and sewing thread, someone who waded in ponds so much

Tom Mann at Leroy Brown's final resting place

that his "toenails looked like turtle backs," the mill town of Shawmut was an ideal place to be. The Chattahoochee was at his back door, and it quickly became his domain.

He worked the third shift at the mill, 11:00 P.M. to 7:00 A.M. Each day he was on the river by the early afternoon. With a five-dollar bag of polar bear hair and a box of hooks, he made his first lures, which he sold to fellow mill workers for twenty-five cents. From this initial investment the business took off. Before long, Mann was earning $500 a week selling lures. Meanwhile, his weekly paycheck at the mill totaled $40.

"The Chattahoochee was my training ground," he said. "I'd catch fish and show them off—haul them around to bait shops, show them off, and sell tackle. I'd also take pictures and put them in the newspaper. I couldn't afford advertising, so that was mine."

By 1967, after a stint as an Alabama game warden, Mann cast himself into the artificial lure business full time. He created legendary lures. For years, his Jelly Worms were the world's best-selling artificial bait. In the early 1970s, Mann's Bait Company sold 50 million a year. The Jelly Worms came packaged in slippery plastic bags soaked in gels scented like jams and jellies—strawberry, blackberry, plum (his wife's idea). As children, Monica and I—and no doubt, thousands of others from our era—liked to slip off to the sporting goods departments at Sears and J. C. Penney just to squeeze the worms and smell the exotic flavors. To this day, I still associate bass fishing with watermelon-scented worms. In his Fish World Museum, Mann displays a signed photograph from the crew of Apollo 15 bearing the inscription: "To Tom Mann—the Jelly Worm Man Supreme."

Mann's single biggest hit was the Lil' George, a tail spinner named after legendary Alabama governor George Wallace. More than 20 million were sold, and Lil' George today remains one of bass fishing's all-time top-selling lures. Mann tested all his lures in bass-stocked aquariums. The story of one of his prized test fish illustrates the extent of bass fishing's popularity, both in the Chattahoochee Valley and across the country.

The fish was named Leroy Brown, a large-mouth bass (*Micropterus salmoides*). Mann called it the smartest fish he ever knew, and he consulted with Leroy on most of the lures he developed during the 1970s. On a sad August day in 1980, the six pound two ounce fish, which had produced millions of offspring in Mann's aquarium, passed away.

Rather than quietly bury the fish, Mann had it frozen so that a proper funeral could be held to coincide with the start of the Alabama Invitational Bass Tournament the following March. Leroy went out with a ceremony befitting a war hero.

More than 1,000 people came to pay respects, filing by the tackle box casket and leaving Jelly Worms as the Eufaula High School marching band played Jim Croce's "Bad, Bad Leroy Brown." Mann eulogized the fish by reading from Lamar Underwood's *Bass Fishing Almanac.* At the end of the services, the National Guard offered a six-gun salute. Alabama Governor Fob James proclaimed the day, March 18, a statewide day of mourning.

A $3,000 tombstone still marks Leroy's grave behind the Fish World complex, which sits on the shores of Lake Eufaula where Mann originally caught the fish. "He was something special," Mann said.

Perhaps such incidents prompted writer Glenn Morris to muse in the *Encyclopedia of Southern Culture:* "The large-mouth bass may have been placed in the waters of the South so that fishermen have a preordained reason for idleness and spending money."

Now in his sixties, Mann still carves new lure designs from basswood almost daily and continues to operate his artificial lure business despite quadruple heart bypass surgery performed in the early 1990s. He remains deeply proud of his accomplishments and keenly aware of his indebtedness to the river.

"I might not be nowhere if it hadn't been for the Chattahoochee," he told us. "It's been as good to me as it has been to Alan Jackson."

Mickey Gillis scoffs at the Tom Manns and the Tommy Mikes of the fish world.

"They make their money off fishermen," he says. "We make our money off the fish."

Gillis, who lives with his wife and three chil-

TOP ROW: Ezra Ellis fishing with mussels on Apalachicola sandbar, Gadsden County, FL; Howard Grantham with sucker fish near Columbia Lock and Dam, Houston County, AL

MIDDLE ROW: Sisters Fausteen Varnum (left) and Thelma Barfield near Ocheese Landing on Apalachicola River, Calhoun County, FL; Ward Cole with bass at Jack Wingate's Lunker Lodge on Lake Seminole, Decatur County, GA; Chad Lesley with fly rod at Jones Bridge, Gwinnett County, GA

BOTTOM ROW: Bruce Covington with bass at Buena Vista Landing on Lake Seminole, Seminole County, GA; Lorell Cherry with catfish at Abbie Creek, Henry County, AL

dren near Lake Eufaula in Alabama, is one of the hardy individualists who still make part of their living as commercial river fishermen. There are perhaps a dozen or more such fishermen on the Lower Chattahoochee and Apalachicola, but Gillis is perhaps alone in being "legal." He has a government-inspected processing house, which gives him legitimacy and sets him apart from the many fishermen who sell their catch locally from front porches, kitchens, and garages.

We met Gillis some time after our journey, but he saw us on the wide open water of Lake Eufaula one summer morning in 1995 as he checked his baskets: "I can remember seeing you," he said, "and saying, 'Who the hell are those fools in the canoe?'"

A third-generation commercial freshwater fisherman from south Florida, Gillis moved to the Chattahoochee Valley twenty years ago. For the better part of the 1980s and 1990s he has earned most of his income off the river's catfish.

"You can't make a living fishing year round," he said. "My wife does bookkeeping part time. You've got three or four months a year you can make a good living at it, but that's about it. You don't ever know what to expect. Don't never know what the fish are going to do. Don't know if you're going to make any money. It'll provide you a living; you just got to bust your ass out there."

A typical day for Gillis begins before dawn. He picks up a sixteen-ounce Mountain Dew at the local Texaco, tosses it in his boat among the bags and barrels of catfish chum, and heads for the lake.

"I've got 100 or more traps out here and know where every one of them's at without writing 'em down. That's why my wife says I can't remember anything. I got all these traps in my head."

Soon he's dragging the bottom with a dredge hook, snagging the ropes and anchors that keep his traps in place, and hauling them to the surface. On the Georgia side, per Georgia law, he uses traps six feet long and made of wire one inch square; on the Alabama side, per Alabama law, it's white oak baskets six feet long and sixteen inches square.

Gillis empties out the traps full of squirming catfish. The smell of chum (a nauseating mix of cheese and soybean meal that has the odor of week-old kitchen compost in August) and the earthy scent of fresh catfish mix and settle in like rural smog. He looks at his fish well quickly filling with fins, whiskers, and filets, and his eyes light up like those of a man looking at the *Sports Illustrated* swimsuit issue. "They're beautiful. They're gorgeous when you're making a living off of 'em," he says. "It's just like being on a hog farm. You can't smell hogs after a while."

After fetching a half dozen or so baskets and refilling them with chum, he throttles back to the boat ramp with a boat full of catfish and the early morning sun on his back, well before most anglers are even getting on the water. The sunrises are perhaps the biggest fringe benefit of the job. He's seen bear and panthers on the lake's shores on these quiet early morning rides and has wrangled gators out of trotlines, which he sometimes uses as an alternative to the traps. In a society increasingly distancing itself from the natural environment, Gillis's livelihood is uniquely entwined with nature.

"There's only two things I'm afraid of," he says. "That's a rattlesnake and a mad woman with a gun."

Back at the fish house, his wife, Rose, and their nephews join Gillis for several hours of skinning cats. It's a thankless task that ulti-

Mickey Gillis, second from left, and his catfish cleaning crew

mately pays off when buyers start pulling up in the dirt drive.

Gillis's is not an easy life. Tenuous profit margins, the high cost of chum (about twenty dollars per trap), and the hard work scare off most would-be commercial fishermen. The rise of farm-raised catfish has further squeezed the river men. Gillis has little respect for the grain-fed farm cats.

"The best-tasting catfish you'll ever eat comes out of this lake here. I've eaten them out of half the lakes in the U.S. and haven't found any better," he says. "I can pick a pond cat [farm raised] out of a ton of fish. It's like the difference between drinking fine whiskey and a beer, and about half the public can tell the difference too. One thing about a catfish; he tastes just like what he eats."

Gillis fights a battle that goes beyond simply making the catch. Apart from farm catfish, he must contend with renegade migrant fishermen who drift from river to river and with thieves who steal traps.

"I know forty or fifty commercial fishermen in south Florida that would love to know where we're at," he says. "We've got enough competition out there right now. I don't even allow a commercial fishermen in this building. About half your commercial fishermen are like fruit pickers. They'll go where things are ripe."

The skinning of cats and the lopping off of fish heads continue until gloves are red with fish blood, five-gallon waste buckets are near overflowing with skins and heads, and the cleaning table is empty. When all is done, Gillis retires outside for a plug of Red Man. Catfish, and the fishermen that catch them, are said to be on the bottom rung of fishing's caste system—a step below blue-collar bass men and well below fly-rod-toting trout men, but Gillis speaks with the pride of a man who has just landed a marlin.

"I'll tell you right now, I know I could feed my family without ever having to go to the grocery store," he says. "I've never been one to work for somebody else. Here you don't have nobody looking down your back. . . . I can do what I want when I want. If I wake up tomorrow morning and I want to go hunting, I go hunting."

As for the fish heads, they make great fertilizer.

"There's nobody around here that can grow a pepper as good as I can," he says.

Downriver on Lake Seminole we visited Jack Wingate and his Lunker Lodge. Anyone even remotely familiar with the river had told us, "What ever you do, don't miss Wingate's Lunker Lodge." Wingate's operation dates back to 1957 when Jim Woodruff Dam and Lake Seminole

Jack Wingate at Lunker Lodge

were completed. With the new lake full, Wingate moved the family's country store and barbecue café to the lake's shores, expanded to include bait and tackle and guiding services, and waited for the crowds to appear. He'd seen the flocks of boaters and fishermen coming to the recently impounded Lake Texoma when he visited relatives in Oklahoma, and he hoped for the same in his own backyard. In the first month of business, he took in a paltry forty-three dollars.

But Seminole and bass fishing were still in their infancy. As the sport grew, so did Wingate's customer base. Big fish made the difference. "If you didn't have a five-pound fish, nobody'd take your picture," said Wingate of the lake's early days. Seminole quickly earned a reputation as a trophy bass destination, and Wingate's campground, lodge, and restaurant began filling. Not surprisingly, his first regular customers came from Tennessee and Kentucky, where TVA lakes had already created a bass-crazed populace. Now his customers come from everywhere.

"I didn't know everyone in the country was going to come here," he said. "I can't even chew tobacco anymore. When you chew tobacco, you need to be able to sit down and enjoy it, and I don't have time."

Wingate's success is as much a result of his own down home, outdoorsman hospitality as it is the big bass of his lake. He makes fishermen feel at home. After more than forty years, Seminole and Wingate's have become almost synonymous. In 1994 Wingate was inducted into the National Freshwater Fishing Hall of Fame as a legendary fishing guide.

A state Department of Transportation sign stands along the driveway to the lodge. It reads "Bass Crossing." Another sign warns fishermen as they enter, "Cuz, They Bit Yesterday." As they leave, the back of the sign tells them, "They'll tare it up, tomorrow."

Wingate usually greets customers from his spot behind the counter pay station of the bait shop/restaurant. His elbows are callused from days of leaning there. As the lunchtime crowd files in, he greets old familiar faces from Bainbridge, women in business suits up from Chattahoochee, Florida, workmen in boots, soiled jeans, and T-shirts, and fishermen fresh off the lake. Florida governor Lawton Chiles sometimes makes the hour drive from the capitol in Tallahassee to frequent this place.

"How's everything, Jack?" a woman asks. "It looks like you've lost a little weight."

"Lord, I have!" Wingate says, rubbing an ample belly that challenges his belt. "I'm just skinnying right down to skin and bones. Come in, girls. Just get out and come right in!"

As the two gray-haired ladies shuffle by, they respond, "That's why we come here, just to get called 'girls.'"

"They serve meals in here?" a first-timer asks.

"Yes, sir."

"They any good?"

"They're not too good, but you can get by with them."

"You got any words of wisdom this morning, Jack?" asks an angler headed for the lake.

"Fling it and bring it. That's as good a luck as any," the proprietor says, producing hearty laughs.

Wingate's counter sits beneath a bulletin board devoted, in part, to poking fun at the Clinton administration. A portrait of President Bush hangs next to a hand-scrawled sign that reads, "The Last American President." On this day, Wingate polishes off a ham sandwich and washes it down with a sip of hot pepper juice as he rings up restaurant tickets and sodas from the bait shop. "It's good for your guts," he explains.

Whether you eat barbecue or not, the restaurant is worth the visit. It is more museum than restaurant. Hundreds of Indian artifacts—everything from arrowheads to pottery to fishing hooks—hang on the walls or sit in display cases along with antique fishing rods, broadaxes, well

cranks, rifles, irons, bait containers, and even the skull of an alligator snapping turtle that is as big as a basketball. Nearly all of the artifacts were found surface collecting in the area around the lake.

"We call him the Sage of Lake Seminole," said Mary Frances Donalson, a longtime friend of Wingate's and a writer with the *Bainbridge Post Searchlight,* for which Wingate writes a weekly fishing column.

"There's two things we never question," she told us, "that's Jack Wingate's column and Sam Griffin's column—he's the publisher and he uses ten-dollar words sometimes. Jack can spell the same word six different ways in the same paragraph."

In his columns that appear in newspapers all over the three-corners region of Georgia, Alabama, and Florida, he intentionally butchers English, writing the language as it is spoken in the far corners of Decatur County like Faceville and Attapulgus.

"Carp and polititions have a lot in common," he writes. "They is always sucken or stirin somthin. The one thing is, though, you cain't do nuthin with a polition, but an ole carp can be caught, bled, drawn and baked and eaten with gusto."

Or: "Chillun growin up today ain't gonna have nuthin to rite songs about, nor tell they gran-chillun bout when they git old. Most e'vem don't ever see a hoss, cow, doggy, train, bus station, honkey tonk nor drive in. It's gonna be rite hard to tell or rite storys and songs about software and lap computers."

Wingate, now fast approaching his seventieth year, can tell a story. Growing up hunting and fishing along the rivers and streams of Decatur County, he has accumulated a vast knowledge of the area that now sits beneath the water of Lake Seminole. Like Tommy Mike in LaGrange, he has used his knowledge to fill his clients' live wells with big bass.

Wingate remembers the Flint River in its undammed days. "It was a gorgeous stream of water—swift and fast. The measure of a man at that time was if he could swim across the old Hutcheson's Ferry. If you could swim that cable, right under it all the way across and turn around and come back right up under it, you had reached manhood. I tried and tried and tried and that damn thing would pull you off. In spite of what you'd do, you'd go downstream. But I finally mastered it. I guess I was fourteen or fifteen. I thought I was something else."

He no longer guides fishing trips, but a host of other guides under his tutelage work from his marina. Skin cancers, a result of years of fishing hatless, shirtless, and often shoeless, have kept him away from daily work in the sun. Each day he takes several breaks to return to his home for rest and to care for his wife, Joyce, who suffered a stroke shortly after we visited the lodge. After forty years of playing the host, Wingate's beginning to slow down.

"I went out there yesterday afternoon. I didn't even fish," he says, still greeting customers. "I just went out there and let the boat push up against some reeds and just sat there listening. It's the most nerve-calming thing I've ever done. That keeps me together."

Wingate's great-grandfather, a Civil War veteran and a part-time preacher, was the first of four generations of family storekeepers. While he recounts their stories, a customer pays with a credit card.

"They'd be proud of me," he says, ringing up the sale and thinking about his forefathers. "Here I am sitting here, and I can sell *bottled* drinking water and put it on *credit cards.* Now, ain't I something? That's the damndest thing I've ever seen—bottled water for $1.50 a gallon."

A day after our visit to the Lunker Lodge, we left Lake Seminole and Georgia via the Jim Woodruff Lock and Dam and entered Florida's Apalachicola River. We left our home state daydreaming of the state fish—the largemouth bass. We recalled George Perry, the Georgia angler who caught the world's record largemouth on an oxbow lake of the Ocmulgee River in 1932 before the days of mammoth man-made impoundments and $100,000 bass tournaments. Perry won a fishing contest sponsored by *Field and Stream* and got seventy-five dollars in merchandise. He never thought of mounting or photographing the fish, which weighed twenty-two pounds and four ounces and measured almost three feet in length. He and his family ate the big fish for dinner.

As we paddled onward, we recalled the fisherman's prayer:

God grant that I may live to fish until my
   dying day.
And when it comes to my last cast, I most humbly
   pray:
When in the Lord's safe landing net I'm peacefully
   asleep,
That in his mercy, I'll be judged as big enough to
   keep.

Rock and maple at Long Island, Cobb County

Sweet gum and spanish moss, Russell County

Cattails on Bull Sluice Lake, Fulton County

Tupelo trees on Owl Creek, Liberty County

Canada geese at Devil's Racecourse Shoals, Cobb County

Canada geese in formation on Bull Sluice Lake, Fulton County

Bluff at mouth of White Oak Creek, Fulton County

Morning fog at McIntosh Reserve, Carroll County

Stump at Riverbend, Russell County

Azalea at Devil's Racecourse Shoals, Fulton County

Morning at Long Island Shoals, Cobb County

Sweet gum leaf on flood pool, Fulton County

CHAPTER ELEVEN

NATIVE ROOTS

IN NORTH ATLANTA WHERE MILLION-DOLLAR HOMES CROWD UP TO THE river's shore and golf balls litter the river's sandy bottom, we asked a real estate agent which of the area's attributes were most attractive to new home buyers. We wanted to know whether the river was a draw.

She took a quick mental inventory—the golf courses, the well-manicured lawns, the prestige of living in a gated community, the low crime rates—and she answered, "Maybe it's the schools."

Her answer reminded us that this was modern suburbia, where real estate agents reel in buyers with the time-tested lure of good schools, good services, and good neighbors. In 200 years, our criteria for selecting a nesting place have dramatically changed. Where once ties to the land were paramount, technology and upward mobility mean that taxes, time spent commuting, and aesthetic considerations count most with home buyers.

Not so long ago, families selected their homesites in a far different way. They looked for water, arable land, and perhaps building materials or wild game. The need to survive left little room for purely aesthetic concerns. In this way the country was settled and wrested from Native Americans. Early pioneers pushed up river valleys, across creek floodplains, and into the highest, spring-fed hollows of the Appalachian Mountains. It was a slow and arduous process until railroads and the industrial revolution began creating settlements in such previously unlikely locations as Atlanta.

The very name Chattahoochee whispers of this early American migration to the interior. The first Europeans to explore the Chatthoochee intensively were Spanish soldiers, accompanied by Catholic priests, in search of gold. They pushed upriver on rafts from the Gulf coast in the early 1670s, calling it Rio de la Apalachicolas because of the dominant Indian town, Apalachicola, which they found on the river near present-day Holy Trinity, Alabama.

Then the English came. In 1685, Englishman Henry Woodward arrived overland from the Atlantic coast and established trade with the Indian town of Coweta near what is now Columbus. The natives Woodward met called the river Chattahoochee, giving the river the name of an Indian town believed to be located near present-day Franklin in Heard County.

In the years that followed, the Spaniards attempted to win the natives' allegiance by converting them to Catholicism. The English instead wooed them with European manufactured goods. Capitalism ultimately won out over Christianity. The Spanish fled south to Florida, while the English gained control of Georgia. As historian Mark Fretwell noted in *This So Remote Frontier*, "the soft murmurs of savages repeating mysterious words of the religious service were no match for a calico petticoat or a scarlet caddice."

The Spanish controlled north Florida until 1763, just long enough for the name Apalachicola to stick, but up north, the river came to be known as Chattahoochee. In 1799, Indian agent Benjamin Hawkins recorded for the first time the meaning of the word "Chattahoochee": "chatto" meant "stone" in the Creek language, while "hoche" translated as "flowered" or "marked." Today many people call it "river of the flowered or painted rock."

The English and Spanish found the Indians on the river, of course, because the Cherokees of the Upper Chattahoochee and the Creeks of the Lower Chattahoochee had made their homes where they found abundant water, rich soil, wild game and foods, and a natural transportation path. The river provided everything. The natives' farmland was enriched each winter when the river spilled over its banks. Water for drinking and bathing came from the river or a tributary. Deer and wild turkey were drawn to the riverside, as we ourselves repeatedly saw during our journey. From the wooded riverbanks the Indians gathered essential raw materials, and on the river they could travel and trade with the ease of a paddle stroke. The Chattahoochee was the glue that held their cultures together.

The natives' presence still permeates the river corridor in historic sites scattered along the river and in the poetic place names that we inherited from them. In the Nacoochee Valley we paddled past the Nacoochee Indian Mound and Sautee Creek, where locals still find potsherds formed by Cherokee hands. In Atlanta, we visited the Indian Cave, less than a mile upstream from the I-75 bridge over the river, where Native American travelers took rest in the natural rock shelter. We looked upriver from Acorn Bluff in Carroll County, where the half-breed Creek Indian chief William McIntosh was massacred by his own people after ceding their ancestral lands in Georgia to the U.S. government. On the backwaters of Lake Eufaula, on a cool, rainy June day,

Frank Schnell at the Columbus Museum

we toured the haunting prehistoric remains of the Rood Indian Mounds.

The Rood site is considered the largest Indian settlement in the Chattahoochee Valley. It dates to the Mississippian period, roughly 700 to 1600 A.D. It sits on what is the most fertile land in Stewart County, strategically located at the east end of a long, sharp west-to-east bend of the river at the mouth of Rood Creek. The thirty-five-acre site dotted with eight mounds was probably home to a dominant people of the era. Our guide on the tour was Frank Schnell, an archaeologist and historian at the Columbus Museum and a scholar of the Chattahoochee Valley Indians for more than forty years.

"I firmly believe that transportation up and down the river was by far the most important transportation that went on," he said. "Practically all of your political alliances went up and down the river rather than across watersheds.

That shows archaeologically in prehistoric times too. Similar prehistoric cultures tend to be found up and down rivers rather than from one river to another. One of my theories about Rood is that it was not only important because it controlled the richest farmland, but in some way it may have controlled trade up and down the river too."

Plying the water in dugout canoes hewn from massive cypress trees (some of which could hold as many as thirty men), the Indians of the Chattahoochee Valley ventured to the Gulf coast and perhaps even farther, bringing back prized seashells, a staple prestige item in prehistoric trade, which the Indians manufactured into beads, breastplates, and ceremonial drinking vessels.

With this trade, the Indian civilizations of the Chattahoochee Valley flourished. Schnell and other scholars believe that the Valley held the largest concentration of Native Americans in the

Southeast outside the Mississippi Valley, and the incredible number of archaeological sites discovered along the river certainly supports that theory. Literally thousands of sites exist between Columbus and Apalachicola, and hundreds, perhaps thousands, more are now buried under the deep water of Lakes Eufaula and Seminole. Within the Fort Benning complex alone, army archaeologists have located more than 1,000 Indian villages, campsites, hunting stations, or resource extraction sites.

During his childhood Schnell glimpsed the last days when the river, and river trade, dominated the culture of the valley. During the 1800s, steamboats filled with cotton replaced Creek Indian dugout canoes filled with seashells, but by the middle of this century, railroads had permanently replaced the river as the preferred means of transportation. The river as a cultural glue, holding strong for centuries, had lost its tackiness.

"I can remember as a child going down and playing on the last wooden steamboat on the river—the *G. W. Miller*," Schnell said. "The one thing that sticks so clearly in my mind is the bathrooms. The bathroom just consisted of two little rooms stuck on the back end of the boat with holes cut in them looking down on the paddlewheel. For a kid, that was quite impressive."

A Columbus native and great-grandson of a riverboat owner, Schnell never drifted far from the river. He was fourteen years old when he visited the river's Rood Mound site for the first time, volunteering with the Columbus Museum, which was excavating parts of the site before the waters of soon-to-be-impounded Lake Eufaula covered the history.

"I was immediately hooked," he said. "My reorientation to the river really started because of the construction of the dams. The archaeological programs in the Chattahoochee Valley began because they wanted to locate and excavate sites before they were destroyed." By the time Schnell graduated from Columbus High, he was working for the Smithsonian Institution, digging up Native American sites in South Dakota, West Virginia, and Illinois as well as the Chattahoochee Valley. After finishing anthropology studies at the University of Georgia, he returned to Columbus. He has worked for the museum since 1966.

Schnell is no swashbuckling Indiana Jones. He has the scholarly demeanor of a college professor, and he can rattle off the names of Indian settlements without pausing for breath: "Coweta, Cusseta, Yuchi, Hitchiti," and so forth on down the river. Much of what we know about the early residents is a result of his work and accounts left by the first Europeans to encounter the people of the Valley.

By modern-day standards, the natives lived simple lives inextricably entwined with the river. As Schnell said, "The primary difference between us and them is that the Indians never lost their orientation to the river."

River cane, the bamboolike reed that still grows in dense, dark green patches along the river and its tributaries, was one of the Indians' most important raw materials. They crafted it into spears and arrows, stripped it and wove baskets and fish traps from it, and employed it as lathing in the walls of their mud daub homes. They made mats from it and also corncribs, knives, torches, rafts, tubes, and drills. They even ate the seeds and shoots of the plant. Every time we paddled by a tall, thick stand of these plants moving as one body in the wind, we thought of the Creeks. It was the plastic of their day.

For the Indians, every plant and animal had its purpose. The iron-hard wood of the black locust made bows, as did dogwood on occasion. Each fall, the nuts of the hickory trees were gathered, crushed, and boiled to extract a tasty oil that was used regularly in soups and stews. Sweet ripe red persimmons were another fall treat. Mussel shells, harvested from the river, became the knives used in hollowing dugout canoes. The pearls of freshwater mussels became jewelry, as they are today, and a sign of wealth. Crushed buckeyes poisoned and captured the river's fish. The gar's teeth and scales were transformed into arrow tips. Deer made up 90 percent of the Creeks' meat diet and, of course, skins clothed the river's natives. Yaupon holly, the caffeine-rich evergreen, made a black tea called a-cee which the Indians drank daily and used in religious ceremonies.

The Indians' prosperity depended upon their working knowledge of the natural resources at hand. Of necessity they were scholars dedicated to the study of their natural world. Sadly, much of what they regarded as common knowledge has been lost. We know more about Bosnia or Iraq today than we do about the native plants growing in our backyards. Such information has been relegated to the fine print in guidebooks on edible wild plants and wilderness survival.

Perhaps one of the Creek Indians' biggest admirers in the Chattahoochee Valley is Billy Winn, the editor of the editorial page in the *Columbus Ledger-Enquirer.* His 1992 book *The Old Beloved Path* celebrates the history and culture of the Creeks and reminds today's river dwellers of their rich heritage from precolonial days.

Winn has long championed the region's heritage, both cultural and natural. When Columbus

Billy Winn on his 1949 Chris-Craft, *Beyond Repair*

was building its river walk, he repeatedly derided the walk's planners for planting meaningless shrubs and ornamentals. Instead he called for landscaping that would feature the native plants used by the Creeks and the early settlers—river cane, greenbrier, sycamore, river birch, and cottonwood.

"I am," he has written, "one of those people who treasures atmosphere and environment to a fault, and changes in places I once knew well disturb me."

We caught up with Winn at Florence Marina, where he picks out tunes on a scratched and dented Alvarez six-string and holds court on his 1949 mahogany Chris-Craft, appropriately named *Beyond Repair.* Painstakingly renovated, the boat more often than not serves as a floating party barge, thanks to its frequently rebuilt engine.

Considering his upbringing in Columbus, Winn's love of history, stories, and place is not surprising. The son of a physician, he spent his childhood in a large home that included a grandmother and several aunts and uncles who bantered incessantly about pastimes in the present tense.

"Their minds were in the 1840s," he told us. "They talked about Daniel Webster and John C. Calhoun and Henry Clay. It was strange. And the Civil War . . . to this day I can't stand to talk about it. Every dinner we fought Gettysburg, we fought Antietam and Vicksburg. We fought the Atlanta campaign. It drove me and my daddy almost crazy."

Unlike many of his contemporaries in 1950s Columbus, Winn refused to regard himself as a "son of the Confederacy."

"We had so little cultural inheritance that was viable," he said. "I'm sorry, I just couldn't fight Gettysburg over again. We lost the Civil War, and I wasn't going to do that gig again. We didn't really have much that I could really believe in. Some of my peers believed in that southern Civil War Confederate stuff, but I just never believed in it. We had a misguided, racist upbringing that was rooted in all that Confederate stuff."

Winn escaped Columbus and his heritage to attend college and then wandered as far as Alaska before returning to Atlanta in the early 1960s. He went to work with the *Atlanta Journal* at the height of the civil rights movement. Under the tutelage of the renowned editor Ralph McGill, he covered Martin Luther King Jr.'s assassi-

nation and funeral. He watched from the trenches as the Jim Crow South he had already renounced was dismantled and rebuilt.

But Winn's sense of rootlessness persisted. He returned to Columbus in 1987, and five years later, his search for identity manifested itself in *The Old Beloved Path.*

"I am secretly hoping that children will read that little Indian book," he said. "What I wish I had when I was fourteen or fifteen years old was something like that to help root me in where I was. . . . A lot of people in this part of Georgia are culturally ashamed. They don't need to be. What I wanted was something about us. What did we do? Who are we?"

There is much to be learned from the Indians of the Chattahoochee. After all, their culture in North America dates back more than 2,000 years. Euro-American culture has existed for only a fraction of that time. Interestingly, Native Americans viewed the first oddly clothed Europeans with much skepticism. The more the Indians learned about white men, the more they saw them as savages.

To the natives, the Europeans' endeavors in home and church building seemed unnecessary—wasteful of both resources and human energy. The Indians could not understand why a man would build something that would last beyond his own lifetime. In addition, the newcomers seemed to be spiritually bankrupt. Winn, who delves into the Creek's spirituality in *The Old Beloved Path,* explained the Indian point of view. "We go to church on Sunday and restrict God to one hour a week. They lived in a spiritual union with nature that was pervasive in their lives and could not be put in any other category that was separate from their daily lives. We consider ourselves rather large and important people in an increasingly smaller world. They considered themselves very insignificant beings in a huge and unknowable universe."

For a people who saw themselves as part of nature, no more or less important than all of creation, the idea that the white man's creator had given him dominion over the fish, the birds, the cattle, and every creeping thing on the Earth was deeply disturbing. Given the current state of our global environment, we'd do well to emulate some of their spiritual philosophy. We are slowly learning the hard way what the Creeks might have told us centuries ago: we're better off adapting to nature than forcing nature to adapt itself to us. And we're learning that our continued survival is gravely linked to the survival of all living things. We can no longer afford our arrogance or our inflated sense of self-importance.

We'd also do well to emulate the natives' reverence for the river and for water in general. The Creeks viewed it with superstitious awe and bathed in it daily, almost without fail, in all seasons of the year, though we do not know whether they did so for hygiene or for spiritual or other cultural reasons. Ethnologists have also recorded the tradition of plunging newborn babies into the nearest body of water, probably to cleanse them but possibly also for religious purposes. We do know that bathing was a part of many religious celebrations and that it was thought to cleanse one's "being" as much as the body. Bathing and the drinking of a-cee, which the Creeks used to induce vomiting, served similar functions in their culture.

"It's all part of that same idea," Schnell told us. "The black drink and emetics is a means of cleansing the insides. So they were cleaning their insides as well as their outsides."

Clearly, for the Indians of the Chattahoochee, the river was a powerful presence in their lives.

"We don't have quite the words in English to explain it," Winn said. "It was not a god, but to them it was a thing that had life. It had a soul, and it demanded respect. It could kill you or nurture you. It could bathe you or drown you."

In our *physical* relation to the river, at least, we are very much like the river's original dwellers. Thanks to our water supply systems, residents of Gainesville, Atlanta, LaGrange, Columbus, and other communities bathe in river water daily. It is mostly hygienic, partly for vanity, and maybe, for a few, purely spiritual. Babies delivered at area hospitals still get their first bath in Chattahoochee River water.

As we paddled down the Indians' beloved path and bath and past their old homes, we imagined naked bathers on the river's shores and asked ourselves what life might be like if today's people required a daily ritualistic bath in the river itself. There might be a special "Immersion Exit" on I-285 in Atlanta at the river and a traffic nightmare.

Farther down the river, on an Apalachicola sandbar near the Florida town of Chattahoochee, we stumbled upon a relic of mid-twentieth-century culture—a Nehi soda bottle in near mint condition. "Nehi Beverages—Columbus, GA," it read. We stowed it in the canoe, carrying it to the Gulf, and it now sits on the dresser in our bedroom like a piece of Indian pottery in a museum. The book history tells us that a Columbus grocer named Claude Hatcher began bottling soft drinks in 1904. Twenty years later he introduced the Nehi line of flavored drinks, which he followed after ten years with Royal Crown Cola. Soon thereafter "R.C. Cola and a moon pie" became an icon of southern culture.

The bottle made us wonder what archaeologists 1,000 years from now would make of our society if they could judge it only on the basis of clues found in dirt without the benefit of our book history. Like Schnell studying the Creeks, who had no written language, our descendants could only make educated guesses from our trash. Luckily for these latter-day archaeologists, our garbage is well preserved in our landfills—and we produce a lot of it. Could anyone conclude that soda bottles were ceremonial vessels or that petroleum-based plastics were among our most important raw materials? Might future generations mistakenly report that we worshiped plastic, wood, and glass boxes containing silicon and steel—something we called computers?

"I guess they'll just think that we were outrageously extravagant with everything—not just with money but with all the resources of the world," Schnell said.

They will also likely deduce that our society was wealthy beyond measure. Poor people (and those who choose to live simply) don't have a lot of things to leave behind in the ground.

In 1990 and 1991, Winn wrote a series of columns about his journeys in *Beyond Repair* on the Chattahoochee and Apalachicola rivers. The stories told of the river's rich history and natural beauty, of steamboats and Indians. Winn says he still hears more about those few articles than any others he has written.

Though today's residents are a generation removed from the time when the river bound them together, the people of Columbus and the Chattahoochee Valley still have the river running through their subconscious. It still fires their imagination.

"For anybody that has any ancestry that goes back at all in this area, the river has got to be a primary source of psychic energy and fear and also some salvation and sense of security," Winn told us. "The river, for me, is sanctified space. It gives you a sense of connectedness—connectedness is *real* important. It roots you in a place and gives you a place from which to develop a purpose in life and a reason for being. This rootlessness, this aimless existence—it's been the curse of our age. And it's particularly haunting in this part of the South. Having this connectedness with who you are and where you came from—this rootedness helps you grow like a tree needs roots."

Oak leaf on Hilly Mill Creek, Heard County

Sunset at Florence Marina State Park, Stewart County

Sunset at Alum Bluff, Liberty County

Morning at Abbotts Bridge, Gwinnett County

Sunset at Riverbend, Russell County

River birch, Heard County

Sunrise at Long Island Shoals, Cobb County

Cracked rock at James Creek, Forsyth County

Sandbar near Horseshoe Bend, Fulton County

Sycamore in mist, Cobb County

Beech grove on Alabama shore, looking toward Georgia's Kolomoki Creek, Early County

CHAPTER TWELVE

THE RIVER'S MAYBERRYS

June, we were prisoners, held captive by the Corps of Engineers' Walter F. George Lock and Dam and the forty-mile-long sheet of still water that it creates. Like the river, we were pent up and slowed down. We were paddling across the Lower Chattahoochee's twentieth-century landscape where, in places, the narrow old river spreads three miles from the Alabama to the Georgia shore.

We remembered viewing the huge lake from the dam on a scouting trip before our journey. We had told ourselves, "There's no way we're going to paddle across that thing." The lake had seemed as large as the ocean at the time, but as we paddled up to the dam, having conquered this ocean, it suddenly seemed much smaller.

Lock operator Jim Watson directed us into the lock, closed the gates behind us, and pulled the plug on the giant concrete and steel bathtub, lowering us to the riverbed below the dam. We felt rather Lilliputian. The lock is made for 1,500-ton river barges and diesel-powered towboats. It measures 82 feet in width and 450 feet in length. The drop from lake to riverbed is nearly nine stories. A few weeks before our passage, Watson had fit 26 motorboats into the lock. We calculated that he could fit more than 700 canoes in one passage.

Beyond the lock, the river flows almost unconfined for fifty-five miles until it starts slowing again on the backwaters of Lake Seminole. Except for George W. Andrews Lock and Dam, which slows but doesn't measurably widen the river, this stretch of river flows much as it did in the early part of this century before progress altered the landscape. Here the river winds sleepy and slow, seemingly in no rush to reach the Gulf. The towns that line the Lower Chattahoochee seem to have adopted its ways as well. Georgetown and Fort Gaines, Georgia, along with Columbia and Eufaula, Alabama, like the river, appear mostly untouched by the twentieth century.

The towns, relics of the Chattahoochee's steamboat era, buzzed with activity when cotton turned the wheels of progress. In the dying days of the steamboat era, Fort Gaines and Clay County boasted a population that approached 7,000 in 1930. In 1990, only 3,300 still called Clay County home. Quitman County and Georgetown on the banks of the river opposite Eufaula had a population of 4,000 in 1930; they had lost almost half of this population by 1990. In Stewart County in 1930, there were more than 11,000 residents, but by 1990 the number had dwindled to only 5,600.

On the Alabama side, the same population trends hold true. Henry County lost more than 7,000 residents between 1930 and 1990. Barbour County, despite tremendous growth in the city of Eufaula, experienced the same overall decline. The boomtown of Dothan has nearly doubled Houston County's population in the past sixty years, but Columbia, which lies just inside the county line, nevertheless remains a ghost of its former self.

The population decline has occurred despite the Lower Chattahoochee's dams, which some politicians and prognosticators in the 1960s claimed would bring improvements in river navigation that would turn the humble Chattahoochee Valley into an industrial complex to rival the Ruhr Valley of Germany. Although recreation and retirement home dollars have trickled into the region, industry by and large has followed railroads and interstate highways rather than river barges.

Caught in the Catch-22 of progress, in which development and healthy tax revenues often bring prosperity at the expense of history and geographical identity, these towns are simultaneously sad and refreshing. Clay, Quitman, and Stewart consistently rank among Georgia's poorest counties, but because progress has eluded them, their towns maintain a Mayberry-like charm. Some residents can't wait to escape; others you'd have to drag out of town kicking and screaming.

Instead of fast food chains and megastore complexes, there's Rubo's Grocery and the Sub Stop, where you can eat a hot pizza from a picnic table beneath an ancient oak dripping with Spanish moss. There's Po Boys Video and a mobile home called The Hair Stoppe, which calls itself the "Home of the $5 Haircut."

Old mama dogs sporting sagging teats lounge in the sidewalk shade of peanut mills and cotton warehouses. When traffic permits, and this is often, they sun themselves in the middle of downtown streets. In all of Clay and Quitman Counties there's not a single stoplight, but there is a unique charm that is all but lost in other towns caught in the whirlwind of Walmarts and Taco Bells.

Unfortunately, the river's quiet towns also harbor vacant buildings, abandoned movie

Georgetown Mayor Louie Edwards with his three-seater outhouse

houses, and turn-of-the-century homes that are falling into disrepair. Outside the state's Department of Human Resources building in Georgetown, a sign encourages residents to "Think Work, Not Welfare." Quitman County has a poverty rate approaching 30 percent. Clay's is 35 percent—the highest of any of Georgia's 159 counties.

In Georgetown, we ran into Mayor Louie Edwards as he was rescuing a 100-year-old three-seater outhouse from the backyard of a town neighbor. A lifelong resident of the town, Edwards works to preserve some of the area's old farm structures.

"My son lives in Pine Bluff, Arkansas, and they're trying to get us to sell out and move out there, but no way," he said. "They may carry me out there, but that's the only way. I've been all over the U.S., and it's just so good to come back across that line into Georgia and right into Georgetown. There's no place I've seen yet that I like any better."

When we spoke with Edwards, the town was anticipating two major events—the straightening of U.S. 82's 90-degree dog leg in the middle of town and the opening of a new bank. Edwards was particularly excited about the bank.

"There's never been a bank in Georgetown," he said. "Everybody just loaned out of pocket. A man walking down the street; they called him the banker. Balkcor's Grocery—they used to loan money. That was the bank up until a few years ago. Everybody did their banking in Alabama."

Following a tradition started by his father, Edwards himself acts as a one-man bank, making small loans to Georgetowners for a few dozen bucks or a few thousand. About 90 percent of the time, he gets his money back with interest, he said.

The town's coffers are kept up by a one cent sales tax. A couple of gas stations with convenience stores, Rubo's Grocery Store, and Sam's BBQ sitting at the western edge of town overlooking Lake Eufaula are the biggest contributors, catering to Alabamians who cross the lake for cheap gas and lottery tickets.

Edwards, who has now retired, began a thirty-two-year career with the state as a revenue agent busting moonshine stills throughout the Chattahoochee Valley. He estimated that during his five-year stint as a "revenuer" in the late 1950s and early 1960s, he assisted in closing down nearly 2,000 stills across the state. Even now he lives side by side with some of the men he arrested, but he was nevertheless elected mayor. Stills were laid out along the banks of the river and its tributaries, and the cat-and-mouse games that ensued are the stuff of legends.

One night I was coming home about one o'clock in the morning on the Lumpkin Highway when I saw this guy waving on the side of the road—he was from some of the prominent people in town. When I stopped he said, "Wait a minute, let me run get my stuff [from the woods]." He got in the car with me and set a gallon of liquor down in the floorboard and looked up at me and said, "Gawwwwl lee, I done played hell now!" He didn't know who I was until he got in the car. I knew him *real* well, and I made a case against him too. We'd been trying to catch him for I don't know how long. He was a slick man. But we never did get his still.

Edwards might have stayed with the agency longer had it not been for a run-in with the Chattahoochee Valley's unique geography. Though it officially separates from the piedmont at the fall line in Columbus, the river continues to cut through the high coastal plain. Unlike the low-shouldered coastal rivers of east Georgia, the Chattahoochee curves along steep, high banks

and carries far into the plain many plants and trees associated with the piedmont. Satellite photographs indicating forest type show a long, narrow tongue of hardwoods stretching southward from Columbus to the pine-dominated wiregrass region of far southwest Georgia and southeast Alabama. This geography shows itself best at Eufaula and Fort Gaines, where towering cliffs of more than 100 feet front the river.

One night in the early 1960s, Edwards was sent to raid a juke joint in Fort Gaines called the Riverfront. There Sam Smith, a black businessman from Fort Gaines, was peddling bootleg whiskey and running an illegal numbers game. Unbeknownst to Edwards, the danger that night lay not in the criminal elements but in the town's natural elements near the riverside establishment.

"We's going down to raid that juke down in the bottom and a car came out of nowhere, and I backed up to get out of the car lights where they wouldn't see me and I backed right off that cliff," Edwards said. "It broke me up pretty bad. I fell twenty-seven foot. Cut a hole in my head, here, broke this collarbone and broke one of the bones in my back."

He didn't fully regain consciousness until his coworkers hauled him up the steep cliff and carried him to the doctor's office in town. He awoke to find Dr. David Weatherby, the only doctor in Fort Gaines, tugging on his scalp and sewing up a bloody gash behind his ear.

Unable to chase moonshiners through the woods because of his injuries, Edwards transferred to the state Department of Agriculture but stayed close to home in Georgetown. The other players in the tale likewise continued to live out their lives on the Chattahoochee. Sam Smith, busted because of the Riverfront's whiskey and gambling, went on to become one of Fort Gaines's most successful black businessmen, running a filling station and renting out homes and trailers. Weatherby, in town at the time because of the dam construction, set down roots.

James Coleman in downtown Fort Gaines

He became the town doctor and, in 1962, Fort Gaines's mayor—an office he's held ever since. He has now served longer than any other mayor in the state, winning several elections by margins of less than twenty votes.

There's no sign of the Riverfront today. In fact, the only thing close to a juke joint we came across in town was T. C.'s Lounge, a ramshackle, tin-roofed building coated in bright blue paint. A sign in the front window laid out the rules: "No Fighting, No One Under 21, No Lotering [*sic*], No Drugs, No Alcohol, No Gambling." We joked that the "lotering" prohibition covered both loitering and lottery playing.

Fort Gaines, we were told, is a town that's almost been forgotten. If it were not for the high-tech farm equipment, the downtown district might look like a movie set from a 1960s television sitcom. As we strolled its streets, we asked the residents how they found life in a place like this.

"It's quaint, it's charming. It's just like Mayberry."

"It's as close to being dead as I can get without being dead."

"I like a town where I can take my dogs to work with me each day."

"What we need is some fast food places."

"I wouldn't swap it for the world."

Each day, almost without fail, James E. Coleman, the town's unofficial historian and chairman emeritus of the city's economic development council, hops on his bicycle at home and peddles with surgically replaced knees a couple of blocks to his tiny office at the oil company that was passed on to him by his father. In his eighty-plus years, he's witnessed the slow, steady transformation of the bustling town of his youth. "Oh, great day," he exclaimed.

When I was young, we didn't have those paved roads, and the farmers didn't have such big equipment, so all of them had quite a few hands on the farm. They all came to town on Saturdays to shop. It was something out of Mark Twain. Saturday was the big day. We had two or three dry goods stores, several grocery stores, peanut mills, cotton gins. It was a bustling town.

I tell you one thing. Everybody's concerned about litter today. They'd have a screaming fit back in those days because most of the cotton came on open trucks and wagons and it looked like it'd been snowing around here for about a month or two when they were bringing in the cotton. It'd be all over the lawns and streets.

Today, of course, there's not a cotton gin in Clay County. Fort Gaines has only one grocery store. If you want to buy a pair of pants, you travel to Blakely or Dothan. The mechanization of the farms and subsequent exodus of farm labor, coupled with changing transportation modes, sealed the fate of Fort Gaines late in the twentieth century.

"When they started building better roads, that's when it killed us," said Coleman, who returned to work in his hometown after graduating from Georgia Tech and fighting in World War II. "Eisenhower started with his road building and put in the I-75s and I-20s leaving us in the boondocks, and all that really killed us as far as trying to grow.

"We could get industry down here, but when they come to Georgia they want to be within so many miles of Atlanta, or they want to be on a four-lane highway. Unless you have a home-grown industry, small towns like this aren't going to get anything."

Coleman and others pin their hopes on the lake and on recreation and retirement dollars. They wait for the inevitable four-laning of U.S. Route 27, which cuts a swath through west Georgia from Chattanooga, Tennessee, to Tallahassee, Florida, and runs just a few miles east of town. Meanwhile picturesque turn-of-the-century homes decay for lack of caretakers with the cash to pay for preservation.

"I'd like to save this old town," Coleman said wistfully. But ironically, the very infusions of cash that could save it could also destroy it. Progress can be like a runaway train—hard to stop once it gets rolling. The path that progress burns is Shermanesque, often showing little regard for the people and places left in its wake.

Just above Fort Gaines on the banks of Lake Eufaula near Pataula Creek we happened upon Janet Standley, another septuagenarian who told us a thing or two about progress.

Starting in 1953, Mrs. Standley and her husband, Lonnie, ran a country store on Georgia Route 39 between Fort Gaines and Georgetown. The twenty-by-twenty-foot store, which connected to the family's living quarters, serviced the small communities just north of town. It sold everything from sodas to salted meat.

"Back then that was all the rage," Mrs. Standley said. "Everybody had to have a piece of meat to boil their vegetables in. We sold everything, and whatever the people needed, we'd order it."

Just up the road, Georgia Route 39 passed below Creddile's Mill Dam and the pond it formed on Pataula Creek. From the creek bottom, the road climbed up to New Lowell Methodist Church and headed north. The Standleys traveled this route to church each Sunday. Business at the store was healthy.

But in 1957 when construction began on Walter F. George Lock and Dam, things began to change. The survey crews preparing the land for the water that would cover it provided a mini-boom for the Standleys as the workers stopped in on their lunch hours and breaks, but the impoundment ultimately doomed Standley's Store.

Pataula Creek and Georgia Route 39 would be under water. A new Route 39, to be built about three miles to the east, would take the store's traffic along another route. Today you can only trace the old highway on lake maps—black dots over the blue ink designating the lake. A

Janet and Lonnie Standley on a dead end at Lake Eufaula, Old Georgia Route 39

Opposite the road from their modest home sits Lonnie's historic childhood home—a sprawling farmhouse that dates back to the early 1800s. The home was said to have been a stopping place for Aaron Burr, our third vice president, as he fled south to Mexico in 1807 to escape charges of treason. The house was moved in 1959 to its present location from three miles down the road, where the water of Lake Eufaula would otherwise have covered it.

Mrs. Standley told us she'd rather have her river back.

"The lake's made a big difference in a lot of people's lives," she said.

I don't hate the lake or anything about it; progress is progress, but I'd still rather see cows and corn growing down there. What's progress for some is destruction for others.

The worst effect it had on us was we belonged to New Lowell Methodist. We have to drive nine and two-tenths miles to get to church now, and it was just across the creek about three-quarters of a mile. I'm just thankful we didn't have to move the cemetery nor the church.

The lake's a nice place to go fishing, but we already had that. If you could have seen the tubs of channel catfish that Lonnie and the Griffith boys brought out of this little pond down here [Creddile's Mill Pond]. They'd bring sometimes two washtubs of catfish and go out there and clean every one of them. We'd invite everybody and his brother, and they'd bring tea and salad and string beans. We had as many as 115 people. It was the best time, and we just enjoyed it so much. It just breaks your heart to know that it's all gone.

Times change, especially along dammed rivers. The Standleys' daughter, Joyce Sellers,

tenth of a mile from the Standleys' home, the abandoned road ends abruptly at the water's edge in the cove formed by Pataula Creek, the double-striped yellow center line still visible on the decaying asphalt where weeds are reclaiming the historic thoroughfare.

The Standleys survived by renting out boats on the new lake and continued to operate the store until 1972, but business was never the same. Today an old "Drink Dr. Pepper" clock salvaged from the store marks time against the warm, maple paneling of their home. Mrs. Standley's well-tended house plants fill most of a room once dedicated to the store.

works on the lake as a park ranger with the Corps. Al Standley, one son, works for the firm that maintains the lake's parks and facilities.

Down in Columbia, Alabama, we ran into more senior citizens. Small towns seem to be the domain of the old and wise. Young people flee to become little fish in bigger ponds.

As we sat outside the town's post office, an elderly woman pulled up in a rusting 1962 Chevy Impala. The back window held an airbrushed license plate that read "Daisy's '62." She stepped out at the curb, replete in a snowy white suit and bright red beehive hat adorned with plastic daisies. Her name was Daisy Helms and she was eighty-seven years old. Although she'd moved away from her hometown as an adult, she returned to it, along with her husband, to finish out her life where she began it. Mrs. Helms told us brief stories of her childhood on a Chattahoochee Valley farm and then sputtered off to her home around the corner. A couple of years later, we returned to Columbia to pay her a visit, but a series of strokes had left the spry, independent woman we'd originally met a shell of her former self. Her stories were lost, much like the busy town of her childhood.

It was a relief to many in town when she finally stopped driving. Attendants at one of the town's gas stations told us that she had repeatedly been rescued from near disaster with her car. The short, nearsighted driver in the sixties-style land yacht was becoming a danger to small-town society. One morning, as she warmed the car in her driveway, the old Impala went plowing through Mrs. Helms's backyard right into a wide, round tree. She survived unhurt, but that was the end of her driving days.

James McDonald, one of Mrs. Helms's con-

James McDonald on his front porch outside Columbia

temporaries, shared his stories with us as well. Born in 1923 and a farmer in southeast Alabama all his life, he lives in a square, whitewashed home with a long, narrow front porch sitting just a few feet off Alabama Route 134 north of Columbia. A grove of pecan trees surrounds the home, while cotton and peanut fields spread in all directions. McDonald was one of the farm hands who headed for Columbia each Saturday when the town still had a movie theater, dance halls, clothing stores, and a cotton gin. The son of a tenant farmer, he grew up bouncing from one farm to another as farm laborers did in the South's post–Civil War agricultural system.

"Sundays we'd get biscuits. We'd eat cornbread every day during the week, but on Sunday we'd get one biscuit," he said of his childhood. He had eighteen siblings. "We wore overalls with patches on top of patches. We come up the hard way. I used to work for thirty cents a day when I was fifteen or sixteen years old."

Aside from farming, McDonald inherited from his parents a tradition of fishing at the river. Every Memorial Day and Independence Day, the workers' only days off during the growing season, the McDonald family would head for the river or the nearest creek, with cane poles and all the fixings for a fish fry. Lard saved from the winter hog killing served as the grease in those days, McDonald said.

"Some of us would start fishing, some of us would start cleaning, and some of us would salt and meal the fish," he recalled. Traditional all-day fish fries lasted throughout his children's youth. As we talked on his front porch below a pair of cane poles, he was scheming to get one of his grown children to haul him to the river for a fishing trip.

He and his wife, Catherine, who passed away in December 1997, raised fourteen children on farming and the semiannual pilgrimages to the river.

"I love it down on the river," he said. "When those crappie are biting—oh, my God—you can catch a boat load of them. I feel better when I'm fishing at the river than at these other creeks. I don't know why, I just do. It makes you relax. It'll lift you up and make you feel better."

Compared to the steamy cotton fields of the Wiregrass, the river is an oasis.

About thirty miles north on back roads leading from the McDonald home lies the city of Eufaula, where, like no other place in the Chattahoochee Valley, progress and the past clash. Development spawned by the lake and the town's strategic location along U.S. Route 431, the major artery between Columbus and Dothan (and the route to Panama City, Florida), have turned the antebellum river city into two connected but seemingly separate towns.

North Eufaula Avenue is lined by stately homes with a venerable past. The 700-structure historic district is the second largest in Alabama and each spring is the site of one of the oldest home tours in the state. Many of the antebellum homes included cupolas in their original roof designs so that their owners could scan the river for arriving steamboats. More than 20,000 cars a day pass along the two-lane divided road here. Many motorists rubberneck. Others, hurrying to Dothan or Panama City, blast their horns at the sightseers.

At the center of town, Eufaula Avenue widens to four lanes, and on the town's south side, the historic district becomes a thing of the past. South Eufaula is lined with strip malls, small office complexes, fast food joints, banks, and, at the edge of town, an industrial park. If a sleeping southbound traveler from Atlanta bound for Panama City awoke on South Eufaula Avenue, he might think he was still in the sprawling suburbs of Atlanta.

Eufaula now struggles with issues that have bypassed the river's other small towns. Leaders are struggling to plan growth so that it doesn't destroy the town's strong sense of identity.

"This is a constant battle that we have in Eufaula, trying to preserve that sense of place and that special character so that we don't look like anywhere U.S.A.," said Douglas Purcell, who directs the Historic Chattahoochee Commission, an organization that promotes historic preservation and tourism in the Chattahoochee Valley. Purcell's office window in a historic home dating back to the 1850s commands a view of North Eufaula Avenue. Purcell gestured out the window and continued, "There are a lot of communities that have ruined their historic districts. It's a quality of life issue. People come to this town from all over the country to see these homes, and it has a major economic impact on the town.

"Without historic preservation, communities lose their sense of place. You can drive for miles and miles and miles through communities that all look the same. It is very important to keep that special character and sense of identity that is being lost in more communities across the country. If we had a referendum on four-laning North Eufaula Avenue we would lose, because most people are more interested in saving two or three minutes' driving time."

On some days southbound traffic backs up outside Purcell's office, and the logjam may extend more than a mile north as U.S. Route 431 narrows to two lanes at the north end of the historic district. Transportation planners, in fact, have proposed four-laning the highway through the historic district, but homeowners and historic preservationists have vowed to fight such a plan to the bitter end. The alternative is to construct a bypass to take motorists around the historic district. While relieving north Eufaula's traffic problems, the plan might also carry motorists bound for the Florida panhandle away from south Eufaula's eating establishments, convenience stores, and filling stations. Like Standley's Store on Pataula Creek, many of those busi-

nesses could be left in the dusty wake of progress. The bypass could very well become the South Eufaula Avenue of the twenty-first century.

Eufaula, Georgetown, Fort Gaines, and Columbia were particularly refreshing to us because of our rootless suburban upbringing. Mountains we climbed as children have been leveled for office buildings and malls. Woods that once held abandoned moonshine stills have been replaced by upscale shopping centers. Historic homes have been moved or destroyed to make way for condominiums. In such places, the entire landscape, and the people who inhabit it, begin to look the same.

It's the homogenization of America. The communities we call home are all on the same track, and it doesn't stop with our southern landscape or even with our country's boundaries. It proceeds across the globe and through the habitats of the creatures who share the world with us. Nationwide the United States has lost more than 500 species of plants and animals since the 1500s. Today another 900 are considered endangered. Globally, the world's people once spoke some 6,000 different languages, but within the next 100 years scientists predict that only 600 languages will remain.

Leaving Eufaula, we paddled beneath the towering cliffs that gave the town the nickname "Bluff City." The cliffs were only slightly impressive, but only fifty years ago, before Walter F. George Dam, they were still spectacular and imposing, stretching more than 100 feet above the riverbed in what must have been a beautifully scenic curve in the river. We could not help remembering the words of Mrs. Standley: "What's progress for some is destruction for others."

Riverbank at Lake George W. Andrews, Houston County

Backwaters of Lake Seminole, Jackson County

Morning at Lake George W. Andrews, Early County

Lotus on Lake Eufaula, Barbour County

Lotus on Lake Eufaula, Barbour County

Sunset at Smith Bend, Henry County

Morning at Omusee Creek, Houston County

Clearing storm, Early County

Morning at Lake George W. Andrews, Houston County

Backwaters of Lake Seminole, Seminole County

Morning light at Long Island, Fulton County

CHAPTER THIRTEEN

SPIRITS OF STEAM

AS WE SHOVED OFF FROM THE BOAT RAMP IN CHATTAHOOCHEE, FLORIDA, we ran into James Mitchell, a lifelong resident who as a young boy delivered groceries by bicycle to a family that lived by the river and operated the old drawbridge spanning it. The family was on call twenty-four hours a day, permitting the passage of boats to far-off Columbus and Apalachicola. The romantic steamboat era still echoed through Mitchell's memories as it does for many other residents of the Chattahoochee Valley.

Before our chance encounter with Mitchell, we'd strolled the streets of Chattahoochee. Oddly, the only town sharing the river's name actually sits on the east bank of the Apalachicola River. We met Mayor Grady Turnage beside a mural on the side of a downtown building. Celebrating the moss-draped romance of a bygone day, the mural depicted the steamboat *John W. Callahan* passing the town's fishermen. Such murals are almost as common in the Chattahoochee Valley today as the steamboats were in the 1800s.

On the river's west bank opposite town and below the bridge on U.S. Route 90 that replaced the drawbridge, we paddled up to the remains of the *Barbara Hunt*, one of the river's last paddlewheelers and one of the only wrecks still visible to the casual observer. Half covered in silt and sand, her 100-foot hull jutted from the water at the riverbank, the rusted machinery still in place. Fishermen plopped five-gallon buckets on her wooden platform and cast with cane poles as we inspected the relic in its fifty-fifth year of rest and decay on the river bottom. Dozens of other steamers met similar fates.

Our favorite story is that of General William Irwin, a wealthy planter who drew his last breath aboard the steamer *H. S. Smith* in 1850 at St. Francis Bend just north of Eufaula, a town originally named Irwinton in the general's honor. Irwin was riding home from Columbus with the proceeds from the previous year's crops when the *Smith* caught fire. When the alarm sounded, Irwin grabbed his money bag—which reportedly held some $60,000 in gold coins—and jumped overboard. He and his heavy load sank instantly. General Irwin's body was later recovered, but the gold was never found. An epitaph on his gravestone reads:

> *Roll on, roll on, Chattahoochee—mad river!*
> *For I thought thou wert created too free*
> *To rob others of a brave friend forever,*
> *And sink all that's dearest to me.*

Memories of General Irwin, along with the tragedies of countless other steamers, are deeply ingrained in the lore of the lower Chattahoochee. Throughout the river's rich history, the spirits of steam sound the most haunting cries, for commercial navigation of the river has done more to change the physical river than any other exploitation by mankind. In fact, you'd have to go all the way back to geological times to find a period in which the river has changed more than it has in the past 100 years.

Navigational use of the river necessitated changes questionably dubbed "river improvements"—a job the U.S. Army Corps of Engineers began in the early 1870s and has carried on ever since, often with devastating effects to the river and the creatures that call it home.

The original federal report called the Chattahoochee a "large vein of natural communication, needing only a little help by the hand of man," and resulted in a congressional mandate to open a channel four feet deep running from Apalachicola to Columbus. By the time of our journey, the initial mission had evolved into a mandate for a channel nine feet deep. What started with the simple removal of sunken tree trunks and the blasting of worrisome shoals now manifests itself in three multimillion-dollar lock-and-dam projects as well as dredging operations on the Apalachicola that cost more than $3 million a year—work funded by tax dollars.

Still, like the people of the Chattahoochee Valley, we found that the nostalgia of steamboats tugged at our imagination. We sought out stories from the river's heyday, hoping for a taste of the 1800s when more than 200 paddlewheelers plied the river, when there were some 240 landings between the towns of Apalachicola and Columbus, and when Apalachicola, despite its lack of a deepwater port, was the third largest port in the Gulf of Mexico, thanks to the cotton arriving on the Chattahoochee's steamers.

Sumatra, Florida, sits on the east bank of the Apalachicola in the Apalachicola National Forest. It is a tiny community once kept busy by railroads, steamboats, and the production of lumber and turpentine. There we met T. Drew Branch, the eighty-seven-year-old town postmaster, marking time in his ten-by-twenty-foot whitewashed clapboard post office. Yellow flies and gnats swarmed at the entrance, which was flanked by a pair of yaupon holly bushes. The building's interior was stifling, but Branch, a town native and a former Florida state congressman, seemed unperturbed.

T. Drew Branch at the Sumatra Post Office

He told us stories of his sleepy town's past and ultimately the talk turned to steamboats. He rode one only once as a young boy about 1920, but the trip left an indelible impression. Spry as a wildflower stamp, he recalled the journey as if it happened yesterday.

"My favorite boat was the *City of Eufaula.* She's the only boat I ever rode," he said.

She picked us up at our apiary just below Hickory Landing. We had a steamboat load of bees, carrying them up there to Fort Gaines to put them on a farm during the summer. My daddy let me go with them. It was nothing new to my daddy. He'd ridden the boats for years, but I was on cloud nine. We spent the night on it, but I didn't sleep a wink. I could hear the vibration in that old boat, and that paddlewheel back there—boom, boom, boom.

My daddy was a good friend of the captain, and the captain had a Winchester rifle, so they shot alligators all afternoon. Alligators back then were as thick as bullfrogs. The alligators would be out on the mud bars, and they'd shoot 'em, and they wouldn't even slow down.

I was like a squirrel. I was all over that boat. In the engine room, the engineer would give me a drink of water. He called it distilled water—water from the boilers, you know, steam reduced to water. I'd get tired of that, and I'd go to the boiler room, and that was too hot. They had a couple of [blacks] there firing those boilers. They fired with wood—four-foot cordwood. I couldn't take that, so I'd go up in the passenger deck and watch my daddy and the captain shoot those alligators for a while.

Then I'd go up to the pilothouse. The pilot wheel must have been six feet in diameter. They didn't have hydraulics then. It was just manual. The pilot had another man to help him steer that was called a striker. When they wanted to make a sharp curve, it took a lot of pressure. That striker would have to help him even though he had that big wheel. He had to have some help—you didn't have no hydraulics to help you. And then once he got on a straight line, that pilot would let me steer it. He'd blow that whistle, and it'd just jar you out of there. The condensed steam—it'd be just like a shower of rain coming down with that whistle right over the pilothouse. If I'd been the captain, I would have moved it. They had two cooks downstairs and a kitchen. They cooked day and night and had more food than you ever saw at a picnic or anything.

The young boy didn't miss the estate rooms on the three-story vessel either.

Every time I passed a door, I'd glance in there, and there was a woman in one of them about half undressed. My daddy had given me a lecture about getting tangled up with women, and I went on down and stayed out awhile, but then I sneaked back in because I had to peep in there again. She invited me in, and I took off. It's a wonder I hadn't run over and jumped off the bow of that boat and into the river. I told my daddy about it, and he said, "You better stay away from that side of the boat." And I did.

In 1921, a year or two after Branch's adventure, the nine-year-old *City of Eufaula*, with its 225-horsepower engine, caught fire at Neal's Landing on the Chattahoochee and sank to the riverbed.

The loss of the *City of Eufaula* marked the beginning of the end for the river's steamboat era. Its demise prompted W. C. Bradley, a Columbus businessman, to get out of the steamboat business. He offered the Merchants and Planters

Steamship Company to the city of Columbus for free. In 1925, the Chattahoochee's remaining steamboats hauled 915 passengers and goods valued at only $800,000. Just thirteen years earlier, when the steamboats were still relatively profitable, they hauled some 9,000 passengers and goods valued at almost $12 million. With the sinking of the *Barbara Hunt* at Chattahoochee in 1940 and the later removal from the river of the excursion steamer *George W. Miller* in the 1950s, the paddle wheelers were gone. Railroads, highways, and the dangers of river travel put an end to an era.

Still, the idea of exploiting the river persisted. In the late 1940s business people from Atlanta to Apalachicola envisioned the river as a post–World War II industrial utopia. Barges and tugs would crowd the river and manufacturing complexes would back up to thriving inland ports. Locks and dams, it was thought, would turn a useless river into an avenue of wealth and prosperity.

The River and Harbors Acts passed by Con-gress in 1945 and 1946 brought the federal funds to make such dreams reality. By 1957, Jim Woodruff Lock and Dam was in place at the confluence of the Chattahoochee and the Flint. Above Atlanta, Buford Dam plugged the river to stabilize stream flow. By 1963, Walter F. George and George W. Andrews Lock and Dams were operational. Enthusiasm for turning the diminutive Chattahoochee near the city of Atlanta into an inland port was building with the proposals for another six lock-and-dam projects between Columbus and Atlanta.

A 1945 brochure put out by the Atlanta Freight Bureau pictured two smiling young adults water skiing against the backdrop of a river filled with commercial vessels. E. L. Hart,

Mayor Jimmie Nichols in Apalachicola with his gift from Mayor William Hartsfield of Atlanta

the bureau's leader, told the *Atlanta Journal* in 1951, "There is an inescapable necessity to develop navigation on the Chattahoochee to complete an adequate transportation system. Longer delay would imperil our entire commercial and industrial structure. . . . Only unbelievable complacency has kept us from having [an inland port]."

Fortunately for the river, today the notion of Atlanta as an inland port is all but forgotten history except among those visionaries who once dreamed of the industrial utopia.

Jimmie J. Nichols, a four-time mayor of Apalachicola, was one of the idea's leading publicists, along with such notables as Atlanta Mayor William Hartsfield and Ralph McGill, the legendary editor of the *Atlanta Journal,* who called opponents of the idea "short-sighted." Figuring that his small town at the river's mouth would benefit from such developments, Nichols went so far as to present Mayor Hartsfield with a 1,000-pound anchor salvaged from the bottom of

the Gulf of Mexico. A plaque accompanying the anchor read "The Port of Apalachicola salutes the Port of Atlanta." Hartsfield accepted the gift in 1958 at a well-publicized celebration of Harbor Day in which Apalachicola hosted the movers and shakers of the Chattahoochee Valley, filled them with oysters from the bay, and promoted the cause of navigation.

"For the next two weeks we had towns from all over Georgia calling us, wanting to know if we had any more anchors to spare," said Nichols, now a real estate agent and contributing columnist to the *Apalachicola Times.*

McGill told his readers: "On the day that ocean tugs and barges come, the anchor will be a part of the celebration. And that day is a part of the river's future."

Hartsfield presented Nichols with a framed newspaper article depicting the changes that Buford Dam and Lake Lanier had brought to the north Georgia foothills. Nichols still has the gift, and the city of Atlanta still has the anchor. It sits today in front of the city's waterworks on Bolton Road in the heart of the piedmont, where it looks strangely out of place.

In hindsight, the idea of an inland port so far from the sea seems ill conceived and impractical. Additional dams to complete the project would cost $250 million, according to 1966 estimates. The tremendous cost, Atlanta's continued pollution of the river, and public awareness that the project would wage all-out war on the wild river killed any lingering grandiose visions of an inland port. By the early 1970s, Atlantans had given up the idea, but enthusiasm for commercial navigation held firm on the lower Chattahoochee. The facilities were in place, and it seemed that the barges and industries would inevitably come.

The Corps of Engineers in 1977 projected that more than 1.8 million tons of goods would be shipped annually on the river by 1990, but cargo weights topped off at 1.2 million tons in 1985. By 1993, the figure had dropped to 559,000 tons.

During our entire time on the Chattahoochee, we saw only three barges. On the more heavily traveled Apalachicola, we spotted perhaps a dozen commercial vessels. One year earlier, only twenty-eight barges had made the trip to the head of navigation at Columbus. A Corps of Engineers study revealed that of the country's twenty-seven active inland waterways, only one other waterway cost American taxpayers more to operate than the Apalachicola-Chattahoochee-Flint (ACF) system on a ton-per-mile basis.

Our seventeen-foot canoe was rarely rocked by the wakes of 800-horsepower tugs and their barges laden with fuel and fertilizer. We paddled down a seldom used and expensive highway for barges. If it had been a conventional highway, there would have been weeds growing through the center line.

The Apalachicola's wild bends, shifting sands, and periodic extended droughts coupled with the uncertainties brought on by the Tri-State Water Study and metropolitan Atlanta's demand for more water have left the system with a reputation for being unreliable. Barge operators and business investors wonder whether there'll be enough water to float their goods. As a result the development that was supposed to accompany the locks and dams has yet to arrive.

Halfway down the Apalachicola, we paddled past the hulking dredge barge Hendry No. 6 and its floating companion, a two-story workers' quarters where some thirty men eat, sleep, and work on the river twenty-four hours a day. In its contract with the Corps and the American taxpayers, the Hendry barge spends about seven months each year on the waterway, sucking sand from the bottom of the main channel and spitting it into the shallows and along the edges of the river.

We caught up with Captain John Cole in Apalachicola some time later as his barge outfit worked the Bay, clearing a channel through the estuary's shallow water to the Gulf of Mexico. Captain Cole has the look of a Pillsbury Doughboy baked by the sun and hardened by thirty-six years of dredging Gulf coast rivers. A computer-generated card on the door to his office and bedroom pictures a mountain goat. It was sent to him by the Hendry Corporation's Tampa headquarters because, he says, he's stubborn as a goat. A native of nearby Altha, Florida, married for thirty-two years and the father of six children, he spends about 300 days a year living on the barge. He directs the efforts to facilitate commercial

John Cole on the Hendry Barge

navigation, work that is condemned by environmentalists, who claim that the dredging destroys the river and the habitat of endangered species.

Life on the dredge boat is insulated from such concerns, however. Once on the river, Cole and his crew are in a strange way liberated from worldly cares. They feel alone with the river and their machinery, at peace. It was a feeling that we found familiar. The crew's quarters are Spartan—four bunks to a room. A well-stocked freezer and pantry supply the crew with daily meals of barbecued ribs, T-bone steaks, pork chops, meatloaf, and, when the cook and crew are in the mood, freshly caught catfish. Levermen, pilots, engineers, and the captain eat together, sitting on benches at a long table. Nearby there is a simple lounge. A television with a VCR in one corner blares choices like Clint Eastwood's *High Plains Drifter.* Chess and checkers are stacked on a shelf along with decks of cards for the regular poker games. The 150-ton floating apartment is fully self-contained, with its own sewage system and its own water treatment system.

"You're free out here," Cole said. "You're away from all the activity—the modern-day world. It hasn't changed out here in years. It's kind of like taking a fishing trip—you're free from everything else. You kind of get away from the mainstream."

Cole first worked on the Apalachicola in 1969, when the river's young dams still fueled an atmosphere of hope and expectancy. Nearly thirty years later, the prevailing mood among barge operators is one of defensiveness and desperation. They're fighting to protect their livelihood from a cost-conscious Congress and the legitimate concerns of conservationists.

"They were talking of putting in a dam below Blountstown [on the Apalachicola in the early 1970s], like they have at Columbia," Cole said of his early days on the river. "But it's turned the other way now. A lot of people would like to see it shut slam down."

Cole chose his words carefully when we asked about the feasibility of keeping the waterway open. He might well have been concerned to avoid undermining business even though he was nearing retirement. Cole's twenty-four-year-old son, John, Jr., also works on the dredge.

"It was a frontier being explored back then," he said. "We were pioneers, but I feel like we're a dying breed along with the rivers. The ones that really understood the run of the river—you don't have those people anymore."

There was a long pause, as if he didn't really want to continue. Then he added: "I don't think we have enough traffic to keep it open dollar for dollar. Realistically, dollar for dollar, it should be closed down. We don't have many boats anymore. They didn't go far enough with it to make it a true waterway. If they had carried it on to Atlanta and opened it like they have the other waterways, it would have been different."

But since the 1800s, the Apalachicola and Chattahoochee have proven uncooperative business partners. Unless millions more are spent and more of the wild river is sacrificed, they will remain uncooperative. The Corps' work on the ACF has become akin to a shade tree mechanic's attempting to create a Cadillac from a trio of Pontiacs. No matter how you alter the parts, you'll never make it run like a Caddy. The ACF, a comparatively small river system, was never meant to carry 1,500-ton barges.

Narrow and swift, the Apalachicola ranks among the most difficult rivers of the Gulf coast's inland waterway system. Only a skilled pilot familiar with its subtleties can successfully take a load of petroleum from the Bay to Columbus.

Thomas Eustus Arnold, who works alongside Captain Cole on the Hendry No. 6 is one such man. A pilot on the Chattahoochee since the 1970s, he's had run-ins with the river's bends, nearly losing a tug in one hair-raising encounter.

"If you're used to running the river, you've got something to go from," he explained, "but people that are not used to it, that current will tear them up. You've got a lot of bends where rock lines both sides of it. If you don't line it up just right or you misjudge the current, it'll set you down on those rocks and tear the bottom off your boat."

The river's pilots have been saying the same thing for more than 100 years. Commercial navigation, which began in earnest in 1828 when the *Fanny* pulled up to the docks at Columbus, has been a series of tragedies in which Mother Nature has consistently defeated every attempt to subjugate the lower Chattahoochee.

Many of the early paddlewheelers, including the *Fanny*, of course wound up on the bottom of the Chattahoochee and Apalachicola: the *Georgian* snagged in December 1833, the *Ellen* snagged and sank April 1840, the *Cusseta* collided with the *Union* and sank February 1856, the *George W. Wylly* collided with a bridge pier and sank April 1883, the *Franklin* burned January 1854, the *John C. Calhoun* exploded April 1860. And that's just naming a few. Their boilers blew, the ash blowing from their stacks ignited the cotton they carried, they ran aground on sandbars, they smashed against hidden underwater logs and shoals, and they were carried away and crushed by floodwaters. Like today's mobile homes sitting in the paths of a tornado, the ships constantly courted disaster.

Author Edward Mueller in his book *Perilous Journeys—The History of Steamboating on the*

T. E. "Wewa" Arnold in the pilothouse of the Hendry tug *Johnny H*

A-C-F Rivers wrote, "The U.S. Army Corps of Engineers was striving to improve the river, but many veteran river folk believed their efforts were a waste of time. . . . the river was continually cutting new paths and did as it wished and many of the manmade efforts were futile."

The ill-fated Confederate Navy also found its heroic efforts thwarted by the unpredictable waterway. The *Chattahoochee*, a gunboat designed to steam downriver and break the Union blockade at Apalachicola, ran aground and damaged its hull just two hours into its maiden voyage. After repairs, it was launched again, but again, six miles into its journey toward Apalachicola, it ran aground on a sandbar and lay stranded there for a week until rains raised the water level. At the close of the war the navy set it ablaze at Columbus and let it sink in the river rather than surrender it to Union troops.

The crown jewel of the Confederate Navy on the Chattahoochee, an ironclad called the

Jackson, was never completed, thanks in part to the river's unpredictability. Ready for launching in December 1863 at the Columbus Naval Iron Works, it could not be launched because of a sudden rise and drop in river levels. Redesigns, including alterations to make it more navigable in the river's shallow water, delayed its launch until December 1864. When Union troops captured Columbus in April 1865, the ironclad was still sitting in port, awaiting its armament.

In *Navy Gray*, a comprehensive history of the Confederate Navy on the Chattahoochee, author Maxine Turner concluded: "Of all the systems to be battled, the river was most unforgiving." And so it remains.

Arnold, the modern-day river pilot from the Hendry dredge, concurs. He told us, "I've run the Mississippi River, and it's a big river with a lot of volume on it, and that can do some damage, but you've got a lot of room on it. And I've run two or three more of these narrow little rivers, but they didn't have as much current as the Apalachicola. They were just easier to run. I've run with a lot of other pilots that say the Apalachicola is one of the worst."

Arnold looks rough and ready like a stereotypical salty river man, but he is actually quite soft-spoken. When we asked him if he'd seen the movie *Ulee's Gold*, the story of an Apalachicola beekeeper from Wewahitchka that hit the movie theaters in 1997, he replied, "Yea, I enjoyed it. It was pretty good, but I didn't like the vulgar language that it had. I wish they had left that out."

The story of Arnold's life on the river is a fitting metaphor for the broader picture of the industry in which he labors. For more than twenty years, he's earned a solid living as a pilot, raising a family of three in the Florida panhandle.

"I kindly thought that I was putting my family number one by making pretty good money, probably better than the average around here," he said. "So I thought that was the name of the game—to chase the big bucks and try to give my family every thing I could."

But the security has come at a cost. Nearing retirement, he still makes the "big bucks" working boats on the river, but in hindsight it may not have been worthwhile for him.

"Me and my wife busted up, and I lay that kindly on the boat," he said. "It gets to be tiring after a while, but then you're stuck. Your family's set up for the big bucks and its hard to go back down once you make the big bucks. It's hard to take a cut in pay, so you hang with it. I probably would have been better off working a job around here and spending more time with my family."

Like the river pilot, our post–World War II generation has chased the big bucks on the water system, replacing a free-flowing river with a series of man-made impoundments connected by short stretches of altered river. We hoped to turn a river into a resource that could support hundreds of families like Arnold's and perhaps make some rich. We invested millions in river improvements. Now that they're in place, it's difficult to say we didn't need them. So we continue to extol their benefits and hope despite reality that we can make this uncooperative, unsuitable river system into an amicable partner in commerce.

The consequences have been tragic.

During our journey, the Lower Chattahoochee was embroiled in a bitter controversy over the 1994 proposal to list several species of freshwater mussels as federally endangered. These filter-feeding mollusks, which dwell on the bottom of the river, have borne the brunt of the "river improvements." Partial to free-flowing rivers and clean water, they have been all but obliterated by dams and dredging. Only a few species survive in the heavily dammed Chattahoochee.

Navigation proponents saw the mussels' inclusion on the Endangered Species List as a threat to continued dredging. Accordingly, they railed against the proposal. At Neal's Landing on the Chattahoochee, we met a gas pipeline worker who had been laid off. He pulled by our campsite in a noisy diesel pickup hauling a bed full of home-grown cucumbers. His rifle lay across the cluttered seat in his cab as we chatted with him. The conversation ultimately turned to mussels.

"It's gone too far," he said. "Man has dominion over all. You have to ask yourself what's more important: man or mussels? I say man. It's not like we're out there slaughtering them. Look at history. That's just the way it goes. The strong survive."

We recoiled at his words. Had he not had a weapon sitting at his side, we would have countered strongly. If the mussels die off because a greater predator knocks them off, that's fine. If a 500-year-flood washes them all to the sea, *that's* the way it goes! But when we wipe out entire species for our short-term economic gain—and dubious economic gain at that—mussels become more important than man. Our survival is not incumbent upon the destruction of a river and the elimination of other animals. In fact, our survival may very well depend upon the survival of those animals. Monica and I kept our mouths shut, of course, and gladly took his offer of a few cucumbers. We're not too proud.

The mussels ultimately gained protection in 1998 but with assurances that the listing would not affect dredging or navigation. Because of the protests from navigation camps, the final ruling was among the longest ever written by the U.S. Fish and Wildlife Service for an endangered species listing.

"It was a monumental piece of work," said Bob Butler, the biologist who wrote it. "They were fearing that this was going to be the straw that broke the camel's back as far as their navigation interests in the watershed. They knew it was hanging by a thread, and they thought this would do them in, but it's not going to stop navigation."

The species in question are already gone from the main stem of the Chattahoochee. Only two survive in the navigational channel of the Apalachicola. With the ruling, the list of protected mussels species grew by seven, increasing the tally on what is already considered perhaps the most endangered group of organisms on the continent. This hasn't been the only river system "improved" at the expense of mussels.

The gulf sturgeon, once the king of the Chattahoochee's fish, has met a similar fate at the back side of the river's dams. Looking like a gar on steroids, it has patrolled the river bottom since time immemorial, reaching ages of up to 100 years while changing little in 120 million years. Its highly sought-after roe, eaten as caviar, along with its tasty meat and a large swim bladder used in clarifiers for wine and beer makers, once made the species commercially important. Sturgeon weighing over 160 pounds and measuring nearly eight feet in length have been caught on the Apalachicola. Before Jim Woodruff Dam was completed, prior to 1950, a mammoth 460-pound sturgeon was reportedly caught on the Flint River. The salmon of the Gulf coast, the sturgeon once traveled far up the Chattahoochee to spawn. Older residents of Columbus remember catching the fish below the river's falls, but with the arrival of the dams in the late 1950s, the storied creature began its decline. In 1991, it joined the government's list of endangered species. A small population persists in the Apalachicola, but the species is history on the Chattahoochee.

Mimosa on Lake Oliver, Lee County

Atamasco lilies along Baker Creek, Henry County

Oak on Lake Lanier, Hall County

View from Fort Gaines, Clay County

Backwaters of Lake Seminole near Parramore Landing, Jackson County

Morning at Thornton Shoals, Cobb County

LEFT: *Detail of cypress tree on Dead Lakes, Gulf County*
RIGHT: *Detail of beaver chew at Palisades, Fulton County*

LEFT: *Detail of arrow arum leaf, Russell County*
RIGHT: *Pitcher plant, Apalachicola National Forest, Liberty County*

Morning at Brickyard Island, Franklin County

CHAPTER FOURTEEN

WATER IS FOR FIGHTING

FROM CHATTAHOOCHEE SPRING TO APALACHICOLA BAY, NO OTHER STRETCH of river runs wilder and freer than the 106 miles between the Georgia/Florida state line and the Gulf of Mexico. The Apalachicola River, as the Chattahoochee is called in Florida, meanders through the state's panhandle undammed, flowing past breathtaking bluffs in the north and through sprawling tupelo/cypress swamps in the south.

Though it passes through some of Florida's least populated land, flanked by close to one million acres of publicly held property in the Apalachicola National Forest, Tate's Hell State Forest, and the Apalachicola National Estuarine Research Reserve, signs of man are frequent. We paddled past the wooden dikes built by the Corps of Engineers that attempt to control the river's shifting sands and seem to stand around every bend. We drifted by tents, tarps, and the blackened pits of abandoned campfires dotting the wide, rippled sandbars. Outside one colony of tents, a family had scrawled a homemade sign on the back of a cardboard box and staked it in the sand. It identified the encampment as "357 Riverside Drive, Chattahoochee, FL 32911." A fifth-wheel camper converted to a floating cabin sat marooned on another sandbar, left high and dry during the summer's low flow. Where a crystal clear, icy cold creek mixed with the river's warm current, a pair of immaculate and mammoth houseboats were anchored. As we cooled our feet in the creek, the sounds of vacationers drifted through the walls of these floating palaces.

Near mile marker 89 (navigational markers tick off the distance to the river's mouth) we heard the steady industrial-strength hammering

Hershel Mears on his Apalachicola floathouse

of metal moving wood. We thought the Corps must be at work installing another of its dikes built of logs the size of telephone poles, but when we rounded the bend we found a diminutive and dilapidated floathouse and a pair of shirtless, scrubby men swinging at the shack with a homemade sledgehammer.

Brothers Hershel and Wesley Mears greeted us, offering slices of cantaloupe and cans of Natural Light beer from a cooler full of ice. The Mears were replacing the subflooring of the house, forcing treated four-by-fours between the quarter-inch plywood floor and the water-logged Styrofoam blocks that kept the place afloat.

The walls were of Masonite—discarded campaign billboards advertising Paul Corbin for a local judgeship. The floor was warped and buckled. The tin roof was rusted and bent, with a gap-

ing hole or two. A salvaged piece of plywood ready to be incorporated into the home leaned against a wall on the narrow deck, reading "Nanners 25 cents lb." Frayed ropes secured to trees on the shore kept the home in place near the shore and prevented it from sailing downriver with the current. From stem to stern the craft measured a couple of dozen feet and from port to starboard another dozen. It looked like a squatter's dwelling in the streets of Calcutta, but it floated.

Hershel was the proud owner of this humble domain. "It's made it through five floods right here between these two banks," he boasted.

"He's a hermit," his brother told us. "He lives out here alone 'most all the time."

Taken aback by his brother's words, Hershel swigged his Natural Light before countering, "I'm not a hermit. I'm a river rat."

Floathouses like the one Mears inhabits are part of the Apalachicola's landscape, as they once were on many southern rivers. Through the 1950s, "shantyboats" serving as full-time dwellings could be found on most navigable waterways in the South. During the depression, their number rose considerably as families searched for new ways to eke out a living. If they couldn't sell the fish they caught, they could, at the very least, survive on the river's bounty. The people came to the rivers partly out of necessity and partly out of choice. After all, the rivers promised freedom and independence. Few if any laws governed river life. There were no property taxes, no mortgages, no rent to pay. The rivers' common ground welcomed all, but today the life of the water gypsies has all but died out.

In many states, including Georgia, the floating cabins have been outlawed. In Florida, the state has successfully eliminated the shantyboats from many rivers. The state discourages new structures through regulations and permits, but on the Apalachicola the floating homes survive. Most serve as weekend retreats or as hunting and fishing cabins. Mears's place is an exception.

His story is not unlike those of the hard-scrabble river people of the depression. When he left his job as a pipefitter at age fifty because of failing health, he returned to his native Calhoun County, where, as he puts it, he "hibernated." Refusing welfare and other government aid, in 1980 he built a shack on the banks of the river and lived off the river, eating and selling the catfish he caught on trotlines. His home sat on property owned by the Neal Lumber Company, which in the late 1980s began leasing it to the Lake Parish Hunting Club, a change of property rights that ultimately drove Mears to the river.

They told me I had to move. I hadn't joined their club because I was a little perturbed at them. They started out charging $250 a year and you only get two months to hunt. Most of my deer kills I killed in the river anyway, because they run dogs. The dogs would run one into the river, and I'd just run to the sandbar and wait for it to get on the bar and shoot it. I killed more deer that way, so I wasn't about to give them no $250 that I didn't have anyway. The hunting club can't say anything about that. It's not their land until it gets up on the bank. Anything they can't post and fence in, it's not theirs.

Noting that the river was fenceless, Mears dismantled his home piece by piece and rebuilt it atop Styrofoam on the river where no one could claim property rights.

I started tearing down my house three days before we got three inches of snow. I'd torn my roof off and I was listening to the TV, and they said three inches of snow—uh-oh. I got back up there and put the decking back up over my bed. I had eight quilts and four blankets and half of them on me. It was three inches deep all the way around my bed. I didn't have enough antifreeze in my radiator, and it busted my block, so there went my car—among all this other stuff. That's what happens when you're poor. I got up the next day and started on my walls. I had to tear it all down to get to the floor.

Since 1990, he's been floating with his motorless home secured to trees on the river's edge in the lee of a large eddy. He's the duke of mile marker 89. When the floods come each winter, he rises with the river until from his front porch chair he can look over the water lapping at treetops and see for miles across the floodplain, as if his tiny cabin were at the top of the Empire State Building.

At sixty-two, Mears began drawing social security. With the steady income, he's managed to secure a truck and trailer for his small boat and make improvements to his floathouse. He fishes for fun rather than cash now, and he's as likely to be found munching on a Snack Break honey bun as on a catfish filet. When supplies get low, he motors downriver in a Johnboat to his truck and drives to the Piggly Wiggly in Blountstown. While his contemporaries have set up retirement homes on the safe shores of upstream lakes, Mears, by necessity and by choice, lives the ultimate in blue-collar retirement for river lovers.

The cabin holds a bed, a four-burner gas stove, shelves full of food and batteries, a portable toilet, and a television powered by car batteries and suspended from the ceiling by a rope that wraps around the console and cuts the screen in half.

"Do you hear any noise?" he asked. "Do you

feel that breeze? I gotta be somewhere, and I'd rather be here than in town, listening to that traffic and people hollering and carrying on. I like solitude, peace and quiet. I might have some hermit in me in that respect."

His one constant companion during the summer is an eight-foot alligator he calls Rascal. "He was eighteen inches long when I started fooling with him. He's over half as long as this porch now," he said. "He loves cheese puffs. He'll chase those things as far as he can see them. He knows his name too. He can be up there at that creek, and I can get out and holler "Rascal" two or three times and here he comes. He'll come right up here and bump his nose. I'll reach over and scratch his neck if I want to. That's how friendly he is, but nobody else gets close to him."

As we listened to Mears's stories, reveling in the independence and simplicity the river afforded him, the words of an Atlanta fisherman some 300 miles upstream came to mind.

"That's the thing I like about this river," the angler had told us. He sported a bicep tattoo and was casting for trout from his johnboat in the shadows of north Fulton County's riverside mansions. "Anybody can use it. It doesn't belong to anyone. It's everybody's. It doesn't matter who you are or what color you are. You could be red, black, yellow, white. Anybody can use this river."

Nevertheless, during our journey, the river was in the midst of what was being called the East Coast's first water war. The question was who owned the river—who had the rights to the water and how much this owner could take.

While arid western states are familiar with fisticuffs over water rights, such battles were almost unheard of along the water-rich East Coast. The controversy began in 1989 when the Corps

of Engineers devised a plan so that metropolitan Atlanta could withdraw more water from the river to meet the demands of rapidly growing suburban counties.

Alabama officials claimed that Atlanta's unbridled growth would rob their state of the water it needed for future development, and the state promptly filed suit to stop the additional withdrawals. Florida, concerned about the effect upstream withdrawals might have on the Apalachicola Bay seafood industry, joined the suit. The quarreling ended in 1992 when the three governors agreed to sponsor the comprehensive Tri-State Water Study to determine how the river's water should be allocated into the twenty-first century.

In the three years preceding our journey, scientists and bureaucrats had been hard at work on the study. It was expected to be complete by 1996. Three years after our trip, however, the project, which encompassed the Alabama-Coosa-Tallapoosa watershed as well, was just winding down. In 1997, with the cost of the study reaching $15 million and still growing, the states agreed to a compact that set up a four-member commission (consisting of one federal commissioner and a representative from each state) charged with determining how much water each state was entitled to on the basis of allocation models derived from the six-year study.

The study and subsequent compact met with the approval of most observers because they had the goal of producing a basinwide management plan. Political boundaries set down in the 1800s would be figuratively dissolved, making the river a regional resource rather than the property of one or more individual states. More than one armchair general of the water war told us that the conflict could have been averted if only our

Steve Leitman with a dwarf cypress in Tate's Hell State Forest, Florida

founding fathers had the foresight to set political boundaries along watershed boundaries.

Our first stop in Florida was the town of Chattahoochee, where we met Steve Leitman, a Florida state employee working on the water study and a longtime advocate for protection of the Apalachicola River. When we asked about the study, he quickly quoted Mark Twain, "Whiskey is for drinking; water is for fighting."

Leitman then fired a question at us that caught us off guard: "So what kind of shape is the river in?" This was the question that we had prepared for him. Though we'd seen every mile, we weren't, and still aren't, water quality experts. But from behind our camera's viewfinders, we said, it looks to be in pretty good shape, all things considered.

"Exactly," he replied excitedly. "That's why what we do now is so important. It is still in good shape. We can keep it that way, but we've got to get rid of that Armageddon attitude—that 'me now' attitude. We need to look at ourselves as stewards of the river. The attitude we need for the river is 'us over time'—how does it work for everybody and how do we sustain it."

Leitman put us up for a couple of nights at his home in nearby Quincy. A product of the 1960s cultural revolution, Leitman has the demeanor and ideologies of an old hippie. He's an alumnus of the Peace Corps. He grows herbs and kumquats behind the home that he and his former wife built, and he told us he thought everybody should dedicate two years to government work in some service other than the military. A sticker on his front porch read, "The U.S. spends more in five hours on the military than in five years on health care."

"I don't work for bureaucracies," he said, though indeed he does. "I work for the rivers."

When right-wing conservatives holler "tree hugger," they have people like Leitman in mind.

"What I find funny is that it's almost a dirty word to be an environmentalist," he said. "What you're talking about is a person who is concerned about where he lives. It's like being nasty to have a clean house."

We felt reassured to see that an intelligent, environmentally minded man was having a hand in the study, but as we delved into the complex issues, it became clear that a "me now" attitude persisted. Short-term profit seemed to override sustainability. When the competing interests made their cases to us, Leitman's idealism was crushed under the weight of "economic impact." The question that was most often asked was "what use will have the most economic benefit for the most people?" It seemed the group who could prove they had the most to gain or lose would get the lion's share of the resource, as if the child that jumped up and down and yelled the loudest would ultimately claim ownership.

Lake Lanier homeowners at the tiptop of the watershed want a full lake to protect property values and recreation. Metropolitan Atlanta, determined to remain the economic center of the Southeast, wants abundant water for continued growth and prosperity. Farmers on the Flint River arm of the system want water from both the river and underground aquifers to irrigate their cotton, peanut, corn, and vegetable crops. Alabamians, harboring hopes of future industrial development along the Lower Chattahoochee, likewise want to protect their economic future. Meanwhile, barge operators demand plentiful water to maintain a deep, navigable channel so that they can continue moving fuel and fertilizer up and down the river system. The seafood workers of Apalachicola Bay for their part want a steady flow of freshwater to keep Florida's most productive estuary healthy. Meanwhile, environmental groups lobby for the voiceless—the critters and ecology of the river, which carry no clear-cut price tags.

The demands of each group, if met, would affect everyone else. On the wide, winding Apalachicola, we began to wonder whether the river could really satisfy everyone tomorrow and forever more. Some of the observers with whom we spoke were optimistic.

In Atlanta, Pat Stevens, the chief environmental planner with the Atlanta Regional Commission, which tracks water usage in the metropolitan Atlanta area, said, "I think if we manage the resource wisely, it can be done. From our perspective and the modeling work we've done, there's enough water to supply all the reasonable uses of the project well into the next century. We get about fifty inches of rain a year here. That's a lot of water. It's about how you manage it."

In Alabama, Pete Conroy, who directs the environmental policy and information center at Jacksonville State University, was more cautious. "I worry about the thing that doesn't have such a strong political voice or lobby voice, and that's ecosystem, biological diversity, and productivity," he said. "I think push is going to come to shove at some point. I think Atlanta can continue to grow and prosper but not without expenses in other areas. One of the things I'm looking forward to hearing more about is water conservation in all three states. There's all sorts of conservation methods that western states have gotten involved with, but talking about conservation is a lot like being Chicken Little."

If the sky is falling, Florida, below the spigot, seems in the most tenuous position. Plain and simple, if push comes to shove, the people of Georgia and Alabama have the first grabs at the river. Florida is at their mercy.

At the river's mouth in Apalachicola, we met Woody Miley, the manager of the Apalachicola National Estuarine Research Reserve, a federally funded state agency that studies and protects Apalachicola Bay. When the water war broke out, Miley traveled to Atlanta to speak on behalf of his state before Georgia legislators. He told them, "Whoever coined the term 'mouth' for

Woody Miley on Apalachicola Bay

the terminal end of the river needs a lesson in anatomy." The one-liner brought laughter from the lawmakers, but when he got home, he was reprimanded by Tallahassee for his quip.

In more than fifteen years with the Reserve, Miley has developed a reputation as a rebel in the button-up world of state government. When the state passed legislation banning controversial gill nets—a law that went into effect as we reached the Bay and that put many seafood workers out of work—Miley, the state employee, was vocal in his opposition. He sports a shock of red hair and has the Irish temperament that goes with it.

"I don't watch what I say," he said. "I'm not shy. I'm emotional, and I'm not politically correct. And I don't consider that a character flaw.

"I wouldn't have any trouble going back up to Atlanta and telling them an estuary is a place where you used to be able to watch tomorrow's dinner swim by. Now it's a place where you can watch yesterday's dinner float by."

Apalachicola Bay is fortunate, however. It still has a full symphony. While other Florida estuaries have been decimated by pollution, Apalachicola remains Florida's most productive bay, supplying 90 percent of the oysters eaten in Florida and 10 percent of the those consumed in the nation. The nutrient-rich bay also serves as an essential home during parts of the life cycles of commercially important seafood like blue crabs, flounder, mullet, snapper, and grouper. The Bay's annual shrimp harvest, which totals some 6 million pounds, ranks as Florida's third largest.

The productivity of the Bay depends on the correct mix of saltwater from the Gulf and freshwater from the river's watershed of 19,600 square miles extending to north Georgia. Too little freshwater and too much saltwater slipping around the Bay's barrier islands mean an open door for oyster parasites and predators from the Gulf. Take away the river's annual winter floods that flush nutrients out of the Apalachicola's swamps and marshes, and the bottom of the Bay's food chain slows, sending ripple effects all the way to the oystermen and shrimpers who work the Bay.

In short, the Bay depends on a healthy, naturally functioning river. When we mess with the river, we're meddling in the affairs of the Bay's fishermen. Because of this relationship, the Bay and Miley, its spokesman, have become the darlings of upstream environmentalists calling for the protection of the river's ecosystem and the cooling of our society's romance with economics and short-term profit.

"Looking downriver from Georgia, you see three rivers. Looking upstream from Apalachicola, you see one river, and that's a much more accurate perspective," said Miley. "It's one river. That's our message to Georgia and Alabama."

"It's a shared common resource of all Americans, but you know, one of the first words a child learns in this society is 'mine.' This is instilled in us at a very early age, and we don't have the perspective that's required of shared resources."

Miley and other Bay advocates hope to keep what's happened to other estuaries around the world from occurring here. In California, the amount of freshwater entering San Francisco Bay has been reduced by 50 percent during the later part of the twentieth century, and as a result the area's once-thriving salmon fishery has suffered an 80 percent decline. Even more frightening is the story of the former Soviet Union's Sea of Azov. Once the most productive fishery in the world, it now supports no commercial fishery. The culprit? Large-scale upstream water withdrawals and diversions.

The seafood workers holding stock in Apalachicola Bay include Bobby and Tillie Varnes. Like many of Franklin County's residents, they have worked in the seafood industry virtually all their lives. Their small whitewashed fiberglass oystering skiff shares the shores of Apalachicola and East Point along U.S. Route 98 with dozens of other colorful oyster boats awaiting duty out in the Bay. The boats rise and fall with the tides that sweep through daily. Like the old brick cotton warehouses of Apalachicola's riverfront downtown, the boats serve as icons of the simpler lifestyle that persists in these tiny fishing villages. Hardworking men and women can still survive here on the bounty of the sea and the land.

Themselves children of seafood workers, the Varneses have raised two children of their own on oystering. They've rarely thought of trying any other occupation. Despite the years of hard work under the Bay's hot summer sun and in the cold winter winds, they look too young to be grandparents, yet they have five grandchildren.

Days for the Varneses usually begin by sunrise on the Bay. They motor out to an oyster bar, anchor, and begin the demanding work of harvesting oysters from the Bay's shallow bottom. Bobby hoists the wooden handles of the twelve-foot-long oyster tongs and works them like a posthole digger. The device looks like an instrument you might find in a medieval torture chamber. With each dip of the tongs he produces a twenty- to thirty-pound load of shells and spills them in the boat. Some thirty years of this regular work have given Varnes the build of a world-class kayaker, with his bulk lying in his shoulders, back, and arms. His youthful, tightly wrapped skin has the color of tanned leather. Tillie culls the oysters, keeping those that are large enough and filling burlap sacks that hold about sixty pounds of oysters. On good days, they can reach their twenty-bag limit, a harvest that will gross them $200. Back in town, they cash in their catch at one of the bay front seafood houses and then return home.

"Once you get through oystering, you don't feel like doing nothing else," said Tillie.

But oystering is just half their work. When they are not oystering, they are beekeeping—the other traditional occupation among dwellers of the lower Apalachicola. The swamps of the Apalachicola are blessed with tupelo trees unsurpassed in abundance and density. Their blooms provide the makings of one of the most highly sought-after varieties of honey in the world.

When the pale white blossoms come in late April, the swamps fill with bees and their keepers, all working industriously to produce the sweet tupelo honey.

"The bees sound like a jet engine when they get going up there," said Varnes. He maintains some 200 hives and harvests around 40,000 pounds of honey each year, carrying his bees to the swamp for the tupelo season and to nearby fruit and vegetable farms the rest of the year.

Tupelo trees are much like the oysters of the Bay in that they benefit greatly from the river's winter floods. A flooded swamp in the winter and spring, coupled with rainless days during the blooming season, usually means a bountiful harvest come May, when the beekeepers remove the hives from the swamps and begin extracting the honey.

At the Varneses' cinder block honey house in

Bobby and Tillie Varnes at their Apalachicola honey house

Apalachicola, Bobby's five hunting hounds vie for his attention, but when it comes to extracting honey, the Varneses are as focused as the bees themselves. The task is methodical and mind-numbing—remove frames, decap the combs, place the frames in the centrifugelike extractors, remove, replace, and restack the hives, and repeat again. When the job is done, the beekeepers are quite literally covered in honey. They lick the remnants from their fingers before rinsing with water.

Between the beekeeping and the oystering, the Varneses have become as inseparably bound to the river as they have to each other in thirty years of marriage.

"I wouldn't like to live where I couldn't see water," Tillie said.

For us the Apalachicola River was perhaps the most pleasant part of the journey despite July's heat and the swamp's swarms of biting yellow flies. During a stop at historic Fort Gadsden, we killed the flies by the dozen and mounded them on top of our Florida road map like an arthropodan morgue. The resulting photo never fails to make us smile.

One of our most memorable evenings was spent on a dark brown sandbar opposite Alum Bluff, a long, beautiful 150-foot bluff encompassing the entire east side of a sharp bend in the river north of the town of Bristol. We arrived in the last light of the day. Rain clouds, which had been threatening all day, broke up and gave way to sun in the late afternoon. The light brought forth a palette of umbers, tans, and golds on the bluff's bare walls. As we beached our canoe, a bald eagle flew over our heads and lighted in a pine near the top of the bluff. A flock of seven swallow-tailed kites soon arrived, soaring on the winds that blew off the storm clouds. Hawks and ospreys followed, and at nightfall, a barred owl started its chorus.

Close by but fortunately out of sight sat a series of the ugly dikes constructed by the Corps. Upstream and directly to our east, the water war raged on in Tallahassee, Montgomery, and Atlanta. But here opposite Alum Bluff, at least, the river seemed as it should be—breathtaking and free, owned by no one but home to Hershel Mears, the Varneses, and a pair of sun-parched canoeists who'd fallen in love with a river.

Sunrise at Blue Spring Sandbar, Jackson County

Moon and tupelo tree at the mouth of Owl Creek, Liberty County

Wolf tracks and palms on Little St. George Island, Franklin County

Moon at sunrise on Little St. George Island, Franklin County

Evening on Cashie Creek, Franklin County

Cypress knee and tupelo tree at Brickyard Creek, Franklin County

Afternoon at Alum Bluff, Liberty County

Cypress trees at Wright Lake, Liberty County

Cypress on Dead Lakes, Gulf County

Dwarf cypress in Tate's Hell State Forest, Franklin County

ABOVE: *The canoe at sunrise on the Apalachicola River's Brickyard Island*
FACING PAGE: *Joe and Monica celebrating the journey's end on St. George Island*

CHAPTER FIFTEEN

UNFINISHED BUSINESS

Before sunrise on our final day on the river, we shoved off from the docks at Breakaway Marina three miles above the mouth of the river and Apalachicola Bay. We reached the town of Apalachicola as the sun broke the horizon, splashing gold across the water. Mist hung in the marshes, while the bright rusting hulls of shrimp boats like *Georgia Girl* and *Lucky Lady* caught the morning light, their stoic facades reflected in the river's dark water. Below the bridge on U.S. Route 98, a pair of bottle-nosed dolphins surfaced in front of our canoe. They seemed a fitting saltwater welcome committee, would-be mascots reminding us of the pair of salamanders that we had fished from Chattahoochee Spring some 3,500 feet above sea level and some 540 miles upstream.

Riding the early morning tide as it moved into the Bay from the west, we set our sights on St. George Island six miles southeast of the river's mouth. The Gulf of Mexico, our final destination, lay on the opposite side of the slender barrier island.

In foul weather, the shallow bay can become as choppy as the Gulf itself, but on this day it was as calm as a spring morning on Lake Lanier. A gentle breeze blew at our backs from the northwest, making the long paddle across the Bay a pleasant task. With the tide pushing in tandem with the wind, we could rest our paddles on the gunwales and still make progress.

The water tower on the resort island served as our lighthouse. We kept it at twelve o'clock and pushed toward it, finally reaching the north side

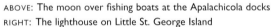

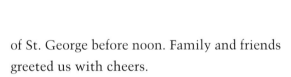

ABOVE: The moon over fishing boats at the Apalachicola docks
RIGHT: The lighthouse on Little St. George Island

of St. George before noon. Family and friends greeted us with cheers.

Noticeable among the group were Webster and Debbie McLain of Donalsonville, Georgia. A few weeks earlier, they had spotted us walking down the road to the Donalsonville post office and had immediately recognized us from a spot on local television. They had put us up for a night at a fishing lodge on Lake Seminole and had invited us to a covered dish supper in their home with friends and neighbors. Their kindness was typical of the people we met along the river's shores. We've often said that if this trip did nothing else, it helped restore our faith in the innate goodness of humankind. The McLains made the two-hour drive to St. George from their Lake

Seminole home and brought a bottle of celebratory champagne.

With an entourage, we carried the canoe across Bayshore and Gulf Beach Drives, while motorists refueling at the BP station stared at us curiously. We raced across the bright beach on the Gulf side, plunged the canoe into saltwater, and then jumped in after it. Saltwater never felt so good.

The McLain's bubbly was popped, along with our bottle of Chattahoochee Spring water, which we had carried for 100 days. We sipped our champagnes—the headache-causing kind and the life-sustaining kind, pouring the rest of the latter into the Gulf.

We like to think a mullet sucked that spring

water through its gills before the bright sun returned it to the sky, where, during some late summer thunderstorm in north Georgia, a cloudburst sent it tumbling from the sky and down Coon Den Ridge to join the water bubbling out of Chattahoochee Spring. Our journey was complete, but for our bottled water, the fanfare of the day was just another brief stop in an endless journey of the water cycle.

We had undertaken the trip for several reasons. We wanted to spend time in the nature photographer's office and to call attention to the river and its plight. Primarily, though, we were following a dream. Chasing down dreams is one way of living life to its fullest. The simple act of pointing one's nose toward a lofty goal and following it with dogged determination transforms a comfortable life of existence into an enriching life of experience. We cannot say that traveling the river's length took any unusual strength of mind or body. Paddling the Chattahoochee isn't

like climbing Mount Everest. It's a lazy drift most of the way, requiring only reasonable health, a dash of will, and a modicum of courage. Very few people have paddled the river's length, not because the adventure is too demanding or too difficult, but because few adventurers are drawn to paddle through both national parks and industrial parks. If the Chattahoochee held the kind of sights and spectacular beauty that we see at Yellowstone or Yosemite, and if it was free of wastewater treatment plants and paper mills, thousands would have come before us. Instead, the river's beauty is a subtle thing often pocked by troubling degradation, and thus the Chattahoochee isn't a must on the to-do list of most wilderness travelers.

To appreciate it, one must find inspiration in its subtle beauty—the way the fog lifts off its surface in the early morning, the way billowy white clouds and blue skies reflect in its clear water, the way stands of yellow trout lily break

Footprints on a sandbar leading to a campsite on the Apalachicola River

A familiar view from the canoe in north metropolitan Atlanta

through the leaf litter in early spring to carpet its banks. It also helps to have been nourished by the river from birth as Monica and I (and thousands of others) were and are. Those of us who grew up playing in the river and its tributaries are blessed with a very natural impulse to follow its trail and discover its final resting place. It therefore came as no surprise that when we began speaking to groups in the years after our journey, almost without fail someone in the audience would tell us, "You know, I really love that river. I've always wanted to do that same trip." We heard variations on this theme from mill workers, taxidermists, business executives, students, and housewives. We have little doubt that the people born to the Chattahoochee's watershed are made to love the river.

But during one speaking engagement, we stumbled upon a question that made us fearful for the river's future. The query showed how we, as a society, view the river and our responsibility to it:

"Are you *still* working to protect the river?"

We didn't know how to answer. The question seemed to imply that "river protector" was an occupation of choice rather than duty—as if, now that our paddling days were over, we could hang up our "river protector" hats and get on with our lives. Could stewardship of the river be something you could pick up and put down as dishwashers toss their rags on the counter at the end of their shifts?

The job of protecting the river and sustaining it for generations cannot be left to adventurers floating down a river and trumpeting a cause, or to nonprofit riverkeeper organizations, or even to government agencies with their scientists and lawyers. It is work that awaits everyone every day twenty-four hours a day, labor performed from a sense of duty and responsibility. The natural environment is our factory workplace. We punch the clock with the lifestyles we lead. We press the lathe with the products we use in our homes. We sweep the floor clean when we discard or recycle our waste. We audit the books as we turn the faucet on and off. The job of protecting the river rests squarely on the shoulders of individuals.

During our journey, everyone tried to blame someone else for ruining the river. We tallied the most frequently accused: the Corps of Engineers, the paper plants, Atlanta, the developers, the jet skiers. No one ever told us, "I've ruined this river," but in effect, we collectively are responsible. It's all too easy to point the finger at big business or big government and lament that they have failed us. Ownership can be too painful, so we pick on the easy targets outside ourselves, but individuals hold the real remedy for what ails the Chattahoochee.

So what can one person alone do? The obvious programs of a political nature are already in place. It is easy to make a difference. There are federal and state environmental regulations, adopt-a-stream programs and river cleanups, water conservation methods, and recycling programs. What's really needed is a dramatic change in the hearts and heads of individuals. For the better part of 200 years, we have viewed the river only in terms of its economic value. In 1802 when the state of Georgia ceded its lands west of the Chattahoochee to the federal government, the state's representatives at the negotiating table did so only with assurances that the river would remain Georgia's to use. Since then, profiteering on the river has grown exponentially. We have treated the waterway only as an instrument of commerce, an indentured servant in endeavors as simple as the grinding of corn or as complex as inland ports 400 miles from sea. Unfortunately, we have abused our faithful servant, assuming there was no limit to the load she could carry.

As the list of dependents grows, we're dis-

Georgia Pacific's paper plant in Cedar Springs

covering that even the river's ability to nourish is not infinite. Our servant's hands have become worn and wrinkled, her back is stooped. There are holes in both her work boots. Seemingly endless population growth and a brutal economic system that treats the river, and our other natural resources, like a business in liquidation have pushed the river to a point of crisis.

Even in the midst of the progressive Tri-State Water Study, as the river's three dependent states attempted to find a way to sustain the river as a whole ecosystem from spring to bay, the overriding concerns were economic—how much each dependent could take from the river and still sustain economic growth. The Armageddon "me now" attitude prevailed. The fallacy in this attitude is obvious: infinite growth in a finite environment is an impossibility. Yet here in the wealthiest nation on the planet, our prosperity reflects this very erroneous principle. The more we consume, the healthier our economy and the happier the constituency. The title of consumer, in our society, is desirable and respectable. Consumers are understood to be productive members of society, yet the definition of "consume" is "to use, expend . . . , to waste or squander . . . , to totally destroy"—behavior that we would find deplorable in most other contexts.

Because water cycles and recycles endlessly, the river will presumably never run out as other natural resources can and do, but its ability to assimilate pollution, provide viable drinking water, and support its own ecosystem may decline. Our economic activity, in one way or another, will always affect the river. If we are to sustain this resource for centuries, we must acknowledge its limitations and reduce our demands upon it today. We must sacrifice our short-term profits for the wealth of our descendants. If the luxuries of yesterday continue to become the necessities of today, we cannot succeed. We must set our sights on the basics: food, water, and shelter and put on blinders to our wants and the lure of convenient but unnecessary material goods. As Mahatma Gandhi remarked long before the first Earth Day, "The world has enough for everyone's needs but not enough for everyone's greed."

The day before we paddled out across the Bay to finish our trip, we traveled a lazy five miles. During the late afternoon we neared Breakaway Marina where a cabin cruiser pulled up alongside us as we drifted in midchannel, absorbing the sun and scenery. The captain stuck his head over the windshield and shouted: "Y'all aren't lost, are you?"

In 100 days, we'd never before gotten that question, even when we got turned around in the islands of Lakes Lanier and Seminole. We just laughed and shook our heads politely, thinking to ourselves, "Damn, we got on this little stream up in the mountains, and just got turned around somewhere. The thing just never stopped flowing, and here we've been on the water for three months and still can't find our way home."

It's difficult to get lost on a river, particularly one that is so dear to your heart. Though we were some 400 miles from our native homes along the river in Atlanta, we felt very much at home in our seventeen-foot boat nearing the river's mouth. Like an extended weekend at grandmother's house spent sifting through old family photos and newspaper clippings of wedding, birth, and death announcements, our 100 days on the river revived our sense of place—the sense of belonging to a landscape we call home. Rivers and streams, being slow to change, remind us of where we came from and who we are. Knowing that we would leave the river the following day and return to our home, we felt a tinge of sadness. In going home we were also leaving home.

The stories we uncovered along the way and in working on this book showed us that our feelings for the river were in no way unique. All along its course, the river flows through the subconscious of its people as its water flows through their veins and fills their cells. Time after time, as we listened to the stories of the people who fill these pages, we noticed a recurring theme: the river is home.

"I suppose if you squeezed me real hard, all you'd get would be river water."

Morning sun on a campsite beneath water oaks in Franklin

"It was a natural thing that I ended up on the river."

"I might not be nowhere if it weren't for the Chattahoochee."

"I wouldn't want to live where I couldn't see water."

"The river, for me, is sanctified space."

"This is home to me, and it will always be home to me."

Three years after the trip, Monica and I returned to the creek of my childhood that had spawned the dream of following the river to discover its end. Like a pair of twelve-year-old adventurers, we set out from Valley Trail Drive and began splashing through the creek as it worked its way to the river. The land around it had changed dramatically in places during the past twenty years. We found a pair of new bridges, and in the pasture of a former dairy farm, a new, grandiose, starter mansion was under construction in an expanding upscale subdivision. On the north bank where the creek met the river, the long-abandoned and overgrown field of my childhood had been transformed into the bright green, well-manicured playing field of the Atlanta Polo Club.

Most noticeable, however, was the change in the land directly opposite my parents' home. There, during my childhood, the creek had flowed through an almost impenetrable thicket of young trees and blackberry bushes. Each summer, we children gingerly stepped through the briars to gather the blackberries. We came home with purple fingers and drowned the tart, gritty wild fruits in milk and sugar, eating them by the bowlful. Now this same land holds two mammoth homes with lush lawns stretching all the way to the creek's bank. The blackberries are gone, and my parents' grandchildren will never know the pleasure of freshly picked blackberries in that place.

But the creek itself remains familiar. Its bends are the same, and the slippery shoals that we used as natural sliding boards on hot summer days are just as slippery. The pools at their bases are as cold and deep. It flows just as it did twenty years ago. Though the blackberries are gone, when the grandchildren come to visit my parents, they are invariably quick to ask, "Can we go play at the creek?"

An ancient Japanese proverb tells us, "A country may go to ruin, but its mountains and streams remain." Perhaps that is why so many identify the river with home. In a rapidly changing landscape and society, the river remains constant, dependable, and stable, like an old farm home passed down through generations. Its smoothed rocks are like the weathered wood of the barn built by the hands of great-grandparents. Its flow is as consistent as the garden brag patch that each year produces watermelons large enough to enter in the county fair. Its rapids and sandbars are as familiar as grandfather's recliner. Its musty, fish-filled scent generates as many

pleasant memories as the aroma of cornbread and sweet potatoes in the oven.

Though much of the landscape around a river may be lost or changed in the name of progress, the river itself remains, never failing in its determined course to the sea. That, I suppose, is why we and thousands of others call it home. It is reassuring to me that today when they deliver babies at Piedmont Hospital in Atlanta, where I came into the world, the newborns still get their first bath in tap water piped in from the Chattahoochee. When the nurses placed my baby daughter's head under the faucet for her first shampoo on January 6, 1999, I smiled. Like Monica and me, and like the offspring of the Creek and Cherokee Indians born hundreds of years ago, she will be a child of the Chattahoochee.

The river still bathes. It still nourishes. It still cools our feet and soothes our nerves. Perhaps no one has described the wonder of water and the rivers that carry it better than naturalist Donald Culross Peattie when he wrote, "There was never less, there could never be more. A mighty mercy on which life depends, for all its glittering shifts, water is constant."

For all the troubling scenes we witnessed on our journey, water's constancy gives us hope. If we cherish the Chattahoochee, it will extend its welcome to the generations that come after us, and they too will call it home.

A rower on Bull Sluice Lake at sunrise

ACKNOWLEDGMENTS

The publication of *River Song: A Journey down the Chattahoochee and Apalachicola Rivers* is the realization of a dream for Joe and Monica Cook. They conceived the idea for their memorable river adventure and raised the necessary funds and sponsorships to successfully complete the river trip. Once the journey was over, the Cooks pressed forward with the idea for a book that would showcase their spectacular photographs of the river with a narrative of their experiences and observations. On more than one occasion, Joe Cook shared his vision for this book with me until I was convinced that it was a title that the Historic Chattahoochee Commission (HCC) should sponsor. The idea for a major photographic book on the Chattahoochee and Apalachicola River System was enthusiastically received by Nicole Mitchell, director of The University of Alabama Press, and her editorial board. With this endorsement in hand, the HCC board of directors voted to help underwrite the publication costs associated with this project. Seeing that additional funds were needed to produce a really first-quality book, the HCC called on some of its friends who share an interest in the future of this river system. Thanks to the generosity of the following individuals and organizations, a substantial subvention was pledged so that The University of Alabama Press could design and produce a noteworthy publication: Sally Bethea, Upper Chattahoochee Riverkeeper; Becky Champion, Oxbow Meadows Environmental Learning Center/Columbus State University; Bill Archer, Georgia Power Company; Jim Phillips, Chattahoochee Riverkeeper; John Sibley, The Georgia Conservancy; and Bruce W. Kirbo of the Thomas M. Kirbo and Irene B. Kirbo Charitable Trust. Special acknowledgment should also be given to the HCC's Publication Committee members who, without hesitation, endorsed this undertaking: Forrest Shivers, Dick Grube, Jacquelyn Rucker, Clason Kyle, Ruth Crump, Judy Tye, Kaye Minchew, Lynne MacElvain, Steve Sharp, and Laura Lewis. HCC secretaries Deborah Shaw and Janice South as well as HCC board member Oline Reynolds also played key roles in this process. Without the dedication and commitment of all these individuals and organizations, the publication of this book would not have been possible.

Douglas Clare Purcell
Executive Director
Historic Chattahoochee Commission

Though we had in the back of our minds a vague notion of producing a book from our journey, that was not the intent of the trip. It was not until more than a year after our journey that we began seriously considering the idea of a book about the river, and then only after much prodding from friends, family, and those who saw our slide presentations and asked, "When are you going to write a book about this?"

There are many individuals and organizations to thank for making both our journey and this book possible. First and foremost we thank Sally Bethea and the staff of the Upper Chattahoochee Riverkeeper who enthusiastically embraced our idea of a source-to-sea journey from the time of our first meeting in 1994. Sally's encouragement and endorsement, along with endorsements from Greg Greer and the Chattahoochee Nature Center and Karen Plant, the Chattahoochee Riverkeeper in Columbus, provided us with the initial support to make our dream reality.

Numerous companies helped outfit us for the journey, and we would like to thank in particular Tom Windham and the Dagger Canoe Company for donating to the expedition a seventeen-foot Passage. Headwaters of Harriman, Tennessee; the Recreational Equipment Incorporated (REI) stores of Atlanta; Pelican Products of Torrance, California; Sevananda Natural Foods Co-op in Atlanta; Chattem Consumer Products, makers of Bullfrog Sunblock in Chattanooga, Tennessee; Go with the Flow Paddlesports in Roswell; Noblex Cameras of Muncy, Pennsylvania; Vision Graphics Screen Printing of Rome, Georgia; Mann's Bait Company of Eufaula, Alabama; and Tom Mann's Fish World of Eufaula, Alabama, also donated valuable supplies and expert advice.

During our journey, we were overwhelmed with kindness and hospitality, and we would like to thank the following people for inviting us into their homes, welcoming us into their towns, enriching our lives, and sharing in our crazy dream: Steve Isenburg of the National Canoe and Kayak Team; Jimmy Johnston and the Steele family in Sautee-Nacoochee; Lam Hardman III in Commerce; Larry and Rebecca Portwood in White County; Anne Gale in Helen; Gary Gaines, John and Connie Hagler, and Dennis Green in Gainesville; Wayne Holcomb, Morris Jackson, and W. E. Pitts of the Georgia Power Company; Howard and Gail Marshall and the Douglas County Water Authority; Chris Jennings and the students of Arnco-Sargent Elementary School in Coweta County; Gandy Glover in Newnan; Scott, Caroline, and Becca Hansen in Roscoe; Margaret Zachry and Steve Johnson in West Point; the firefighters of West Point; Dennis Locke in Phenix City; the Columbus Hilton; Staci Bence in Atlanta; Frank Schnell and Neal Wickham in Columbus; the staffs at Florence Marina and Seminole State Parks in Georgia and Lakepoint Resort Park in Alabama; WULA radio station in Eufaula; Charlie Platt and Mindy Jung of WDHN-TV in Dothan; Lorell Cherry of Headland; Jimmy Taylor of Blakely; Bruce Covington of Donalsonville; Webster and Debbie McLain and all the good folks around Trails End Marina; Jack Wingate on Lake Seminole; Steve Leitman in Quincy; Jerry Kelley and family in Wewahitchka; T. Drew Branch in Sumatra; and Woody Miley in Apalachicola. And finally a special thanks to those many unnamed individuals who assisted us in some small way during the journey. Your kindness will never be forgotten.

After the journey, several individuals and businesses assisted us in completing our work for this book, including E-6 Lab of Atlanta, which developed all our color slide film; the Automated Darkroom in Atlanta, which provided financial support for our initial postjourney educational photo exhibits; and friends Russell McClanahan and Ken Parkinson, who accompanied us on several paddling trips to shoot additional photos. The Shorter College Art Department in Rome generously permitted us the use of their black-and-white darkroom during the frantic months leading up to our first publication deadline, and our journalism instructor at Berry College, Dr. Kathy McKee, offered timely advice during the publication process. Photographers Craig and Keri Tanner of Atlanta assisted us in making the final edit of our landscape images. Friends Frank Logue and Buddy Long traveled long distances to photograph us beginning and completing our trip, and some of their photographs are included in this book.

The animals pictured in chapter nine were photographed in captivity, and we thank the following people for permitting us to photograph their critters: Hope and Tom Bennett of Wildlife Wonders in Cleveland, Georgia; Mark Long and Beth McKinney of the Chattahoochee Nature Center; Ron Shinnick of the University of Georgia Cohutta Fishery in Cohutta; and Curt Snider of Wild Animal Safari in Pine Mountain, Georgia. No animals were injured or harmed in the making of these photographs; however, one human, Beth McKinney, was bitten on the leg by one of the Nature Center's beavers.

This book would not have been possible without the direction of Doug Purcell and the Historic Chattahoochee Commission, who gathered additional funding for the book's publication and guided us through the first stages of the publishing process. At The University of Alabama Press, we thank Nicole Mitchell and her staff for sharing our vision of a coffee-table book filled throughout with both words and photos. And special thanks to Pete Conroy of Jacksonville State University who first advised us to pitch our book idea to The University of Alabama Press.

Joe and Monica Cook
Rome, Georgia

NOTES ON PHOTOGRAPHS

Photographs for this book were shot with two Nikon FM2 35mm cameras. Several Nikon lenses were employed, including a 28mm, 50mm, 105mm, and 180mm as well as a Nikon close-up diopter. The panoramic images were shot using a Noblex 35mm camera with a rotating lens that produces 136-degree views and film images measuring 24mm x 66mm, or roughly the size of two normal 35mm transparencies.

Fujichrome 100 slide film was used exclusively for the color images, and Kodak T-Max 400 film was used for the black-and-white images. Black-and-white prints were made using Kodak Polycontrast III paper. Our slide film was processed by E-6 Lab of Atlanta.

Light metering was done using the in-camera meters on the Nikon FM2s.

With the exception of a handful of images shot from the canoe, Slik and Bogen tripods were used to steady the cameras during exposures. Cameras were protected during the journey, and subsequent river journeys, using watertight carry cases made by Pelican Products.

▪▪

Limited edition prints of the images included in this book are available in various sizes. For more information, contact Joe and Monica Cook at 303 East 5th Avenue, Rome, Georgia 30161 or (706) 235-1170 or via the internet at <www.artfamily.com>.

© Lindsay Garrett

ABOUT THE AUTHORS/PHOTOGRAPHERS

Joe and Monica Cook are self-employed photographers and writers who exhibit their nature and landscape images at outdoor art shows and galleries throughout the eastern United States.

Joe worked as a newspaper photographer and reporter, and Monica, who was trained as a horticulturist, managed a one-hour photo lab, before setting out to hike the Appalachian Trail in 1991. Upon completing the 2,000-mile length of the Trail, the couple began their careers as landscape photographers.

They are avid hikers and canoeists and continue to document both the Appalachian Trail and the Chattahoochee.

Their photographs have been published in numerous books, including *Wildflowers of the Appalachian Trail,* as well as in many regional and national magazines.

Both graduates of Berry College, they currently reside in Rome, Georgia, in a century-old home with their daughter, Ramsey, and three cats.